EVOLUTION *to* EXCELLENCE

COVER IMAGES (FRONT: TOP TO BOTTOM)

This is the original Delmar Public School (now the Town Hall). It opened in 1926 and housed the town's first high school (courtesy Town of Bethlehem).

The construction of the new junior/senior high in Delmar was newsworthy in 1933. The distinct front windows are easily recognizable (courtesy *Times Union*).

This is the third, and newest, of Bethlehem's three high schools. Note it says "Bethlehem Central Senior High School." The school on Kenwood Avenue was exclusively a junior high until it became a middle school in the late 1960s (courtesy BC Class of 1961 website).

COVER IMAGES (BACK: LEFT, TOP RIGHT, BOTTOM RIGHT)

The 1954 new high school. The school is so new there isn't any lettering on it. (courtesy Adrian Brisee '74).

The new junior/senior high school, circa 1936 (courtesy *Oriole* yearbook).

Original Bethlehem Center School in front of the newer school built in 1925 (courtesy Town of Bethlehem).

EVOLUTION *to* EXCELLENCE

Bethlehem Central School District's First Fifty Years

BETH ANDERSON

Evolution to Excellence: Bethlehem Central School District's First Fifty Years
Copyright © 2024 by Beth Anderson

All rights reserved. No part of this book may be used or reproduced in any form, electronic or mechanical, including photocopying, recording, or scanning into any information storage and retrieval system, without written permission from the author except in the case of brief quotation embodied in critical articles and reviews.

BOOK DESIGN BY The Troy Book Makers

Printed in the United States of America
The Troy Book Makers • Troy, New York • thetroybookmakers.com

To order additional copies of this title, contact your favorite local bookstore or visit www.shoptbmbooks.com

ISBN: 978-1-61468-888-4

DEDICATION

*To the one teacher who has had a profound influence on my life
and continues to teach me so much,* **Charlotte Anderson.**
I'm proud to address her as "Mom."

---

*And to all the hard-working teachers everywhere,
your dedication in these challenging times is immeasurable.
You make a deep impact on students.*

TABLE OF CONTENTS

CHAPTER 1	The Foundation	1
CHAPTER 2	Delmar School	9
CHAPTER 3	Elsmere School	27
CHAPTER 4	Clarksville School	35
CHAPTER 5	Slingerlands School	49
CHAPTER 6	Glenmont School	63
CHAPTER 7	Hamagrael School	75
CHAPTER 8	332 Kenwood Avenue	95
CHAPTER 9	700 Delaware Avenue	111
CHAPTER 10	Student Life	129
Afterword		148
Bibliography		152
Index		155

FIGURE 1-1 Town of Bethlehem seal
(courtesy Town of Bethlehem)

CHAPTER 1

THE FOUNDATION

IN THE EARLY PART OF THE TWENTIETH CENTURY, the Town of Bethlehem was known primarily for farming and for its supply of molding sand. Molding sand was used in the metal-casting process. During the first quarter of the century the population throughout the town hovered between 4,000 and 4,500 people. The town, incorporated in 1793, retained an active form of government (Figure 1-1).

Bethlehem was initially formed, by an act of the New York State Legislature in 1793, from a large parcel of land known as Watervliet. Within the country at large, the break from England and the formation of states resulted in legislation aimed to increase the "effectiveness of local government." The position of supervisor, both at the county and town levels, was created mainly to deal with financial responsibilities; however, as the population grew the duties increased.

As the twentieth century dawned, the town was comprised of many hamlets: Kenwood, Glenmont, Van Wie's Point, Cedar Hill, Karlsfeld, Hurstville, North Bethlehem, Slingerlands, Delmar, Elsmere, and Normansville. Within Albany County each town was granted the ability to create a school district. The term "school district" in those days usually signified a one-room, or slightly larger, schoolhouse. As such, the town of Bethlehem welcomed the twentieth century with fifteen school districts (Figure 1-2).

Each district was responsible for its school's maintenance as well as supplying the teacher. A teacher was responsible for opening and

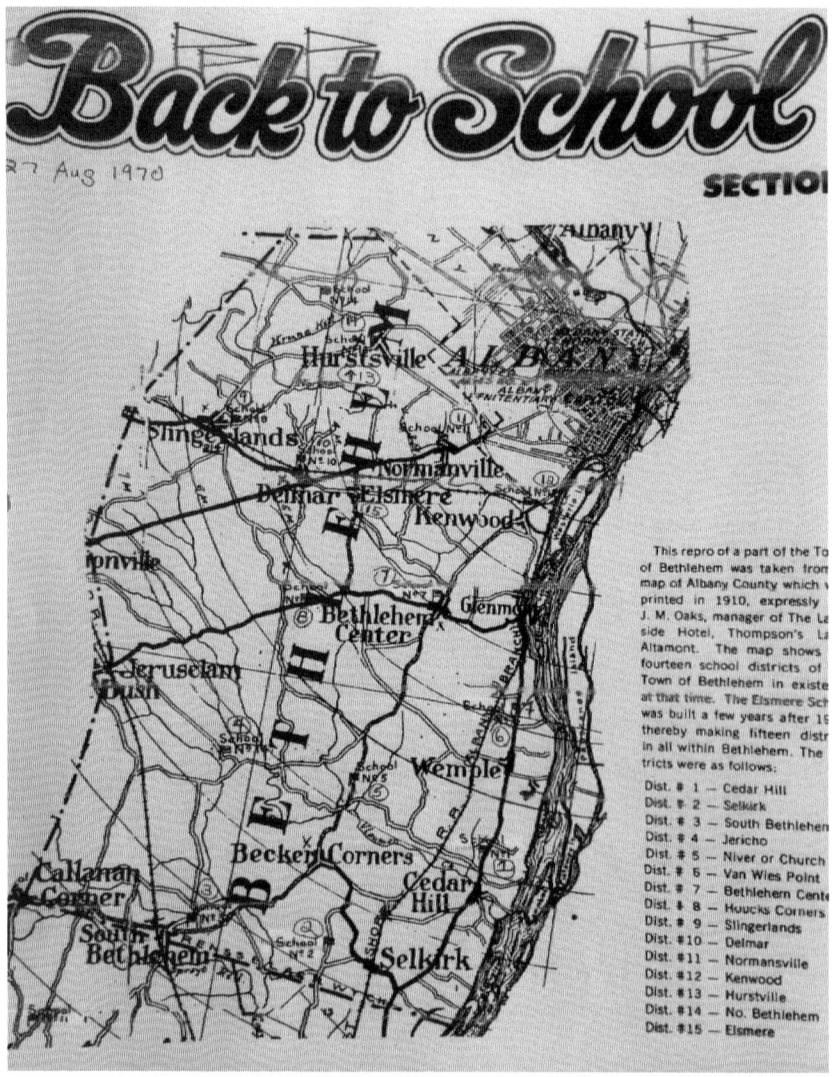

FIGURE 1-2 Map of the fifteen common schools prior to centralization (courtesy *The Spotlight*)

closing the school each day. To that end, firewood needed to be carried, stacked, and fed to the iron stove. At least one outhouse existed outside of each school for the comfort of everyone. More than likely there were two outhouses, one for each gender. Approaching the turn of the century, Bethlehem's combined school districts were serving about 800 students. A total of twenty teachers were employed. Therefore, each teacher was responsible for teaching close to forty students ranging in age from 6 to 13 years. Salaries in those days ranged from $290 to $520 per year.

As democracy flourished through the newly formed United States, schools popped up within communities. Most schools were called "common schools." These schools offered children of any means a chance for basic education, usually through the sixth or eighth grade. This was in response to the many private academies that had sprung up, schools that charged tuition were geared toward the wealthy.

Due to the fact that the United States was largely an agrarian society at the time of its independence, it is not surprising that less than 25 percent of eligible children were in school during any given year. Most children, both male and female, were needed to do household and farm chores. It was a fortunate child who could attend school each day during the school year. Many of the private academies catered to the children of the wealthy and prepared them for higher learning or for a place in society.

The concept of the common school system grew exponentially once states began passing legislation making the education of children compulsory. This movement began in Massachusetts and swept throughout the country during the mid-1850s. Within states and counties individual school districts could be established. The citizens living in each respective district were responsible for the levying and collecting of the monies necessary to maintain each schoolhouse and its expenses.

Integral to the success of the common schools was the guarantee of the quality of teacher preparation. New York State put this into practice in 1844 when the state's first normal school opened in Albany. Normal schools were state-funded schools dedicated to training teachers. In fact, many Normal schools formed the roots of state university college systems. This is true for New York (Figure 1-3).

Twenty-nine prospective teachers were in attendance when the school opened. Provisions were then made throughout the country to establish this type of "teacher institute." These schools allowed practicing teachers to gain new ideas in education. Some of the schools also

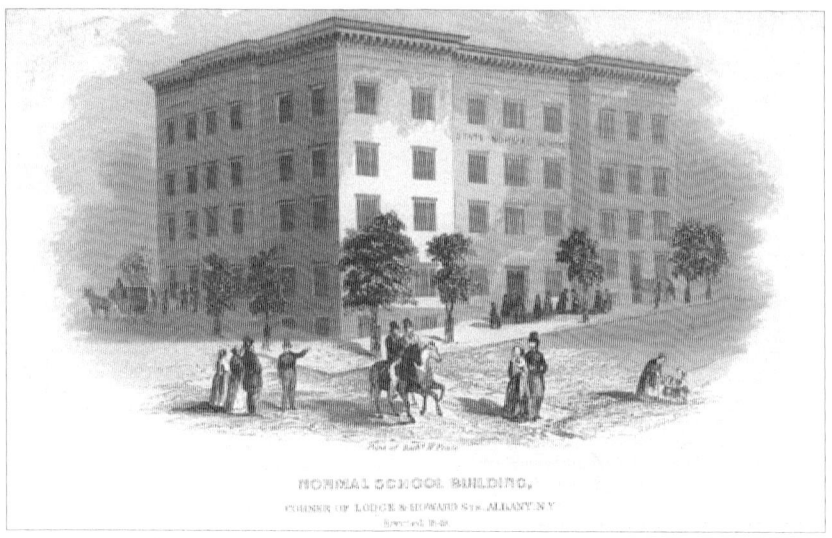

FIGURE 1-3 Albany Normal School, now the State University at Albany (courtesy *www.albany.edu*)

FIGURE 1-4 Milne School (courtesy www.albany.edu)

had "laboratory schools" in which children were taught by practicing teachers under the tutelage of credentialed teachers. The Milne School in Albany was one such school (Figure 1-4).

The first reference to a school within Bethlehem is to a structure built of logs in 1720 at the Nicoll farm near the Hudson River. Almost one hundred years later, according to former town historian

FIGURE 1-5 District No. 1, Cedar Hill Schoolhouse
(courtesy Bethlehem Historical Association)

Allison Bennett, "When the Clermont steamed up the Hudson River, the scholars were allowed to go to the riverbank and watch the boat's passage." To this day most of us can recall momentous events that occurred during our school years. Though this was the first school built within the town's confines, the building that eventually became School District No. 1 was the Cedar Hill School.

Built in 1859, the Cedar Hill School began its life as a one-room schoolhouse. In the early 1900s it was expanded to two rooms. This school remained in use until 1962, when the centralization of schools caused it to close. To this day, it remains as it looked when used as a schoolhouse and is now owned by the Town of Bethlehem. Known as the Little Red Schoolhouse, it serves as the museum for the Bethlehem Historical Association (Figure 1-5).

However successful the Common School system was for the primary grade levels, it did not lend itself to more advanced secondary education. Most common schools provided an education through sixth

FIGURE 1-6 Mr. W. Jack Weaver, key proponent of school centralization (courtesy *The Spotlight*)

or eighth grade. Even though it could be argued that students in those days received a far more comprehensive education, any wishing to advance further had to seek out private academies or high schools within larger cities. The Town of Bethlehem answered the call for continued education when Delmar High opened at the beginning of the 1926–27 school year. Prior to this, students often had to take the train into Albany to attend either Albany High, Albany Academy, Christian Brothers Academy, or Milne.

During the 1920s there was a nationwide movement for people to move out of cities to provide their children with fresh air and with space to play. In the latter part of the 1920s construction began on a new Delaware Avenue bridge. This paved the way for much easier access between Delmar and Albany and allowed for a sizable increase in population. An increase in population resulted in the need for expanded school buildings and programs.

The decade of the 1920s, with its economic success and population expansion, allowed for the development of new ideas within the field of education. Since the economy of the country was less influenced by dependence on agriculture, the Common School system was becoming obsolete in many areas. Soon it would make sense for many single schools within a town to centralize and share expenses. A strong advocate for school centralization within the Town of Bethlehem was a resident named Mr. Jack Weaver (Figure 1-6). Mr. Weaver worked for the State Education Department as the supervisor of Agricultural Education throughout the state. In his travels to many areas within the state, he saw firsthand how centralization benefited areas like the Town of Bethlehem. It easily allowed one-room schools to pool resources and share larger expenses for the benefit of the children. The citizens of the town voted to centralize, and this went into effect in 1930. It would take less than two decades for the Bethlehem Central School District to evolve into a district of excellence.

FIGURE 2-1 Early Delmar School (District No. 10), circa 1906 (courtesy Town of Bethlehem)

CHAPTER 2

DELMAR SCHOOL

IF ONE WERE TO ASK A SIMPLE QUESTION SUCH AS "Where was Delmar School located?" of many town residents under the age of 60, it would result in puzzled looks. Delmar School? There was a Delmar School? There was indeed a Delmar School, and it is remembered fondly by its former students.

Just as each little community within the town had its own common school back in the 1800s, so did Delmar. A rustic, one-room schoolhouse was in the vicinity of the present-day intersection of Kenwood Avenue and Adams Street. The current occupant of that corner, the Masonic Temple, inhabits one of the former school buildings, though the original school was much smaller. For decades, a one-room schoolhouse provided education to many Delmar children. In 1907 the school was deemed too small (Figure 2-1).

The community rallied and a new school was built in time to begin the 1908 school year. The townspeople were proud of their new four-room schoolhouse, with several proclaiming that it would be the last school that would ever have to be built in Delmar. Naturally, these famous last words would not hold true as more construction would take place over the years to meet the district's expanding needs.

The May 3, 1907, issue of the *Altamont Enterprise* reported the residents of School District No. 10 (Delmar) had voted in favor of "...a new and modern school building to replace the one which has outgrown its usefulness." The article also noted the $9700 cost was approved by a vote

FIGURE 2-2 Delmar School (District No. 10), circa 1913. This is the "new" school. The school still stands at the corner of Kenwood Avenue and Adams Street. The photo provider's mother, Ruth Wheeler Coates, stands at the far right, second row from the bottom (courtesy Nancy Ruth Hoffman '60).

of 77 to 37, "despite the obstructive tactics of the nonprogressive minority." Most of the residents in the town were pleased, as it was felt "a better and more hygienic school building" was long overdue (Figure 2-2).

At the close of the school year in June 1908, the small brick school building was torn down and replaced with a larger two-story wooden building. Quoted in a *Spotlight* article from August 14, 1983, longtime Delmar resident Walter "Jimmie" Kunz said, "Going to school in the new building was 'really living.' All of the facilities were inside, including a furnace for heat." Prior to that drinking water and toilet facilities were located outside and wood stoves provided the heat. Jimmie also recalled traveling to school through the orchards located in the vicinity of the present day Four Corners.

Even though the large four-room school was a vast improvement, it only allowed for the instruction of students in grades 1 through 8. Stu-

FIGURE 2-3 Looking down present-day Adams Street from Hudson Avenue. Delmar Train Station is on the left. Delmar School would be down the road on the right (courtesy the *Albany Times Union*)

dents wishing to pursue education past the eighth grade were required to go to Albany (Albany High or Milne) or to Ravena. Train travel was the most efficient way for students to reach their destination (Figure 2-3).

Population continued its upward trend in Delmar, largely due to the convenience of the railroad. Many families were interested in moving away from the cities, where dirt and congestion were major contributors to health issues. Delmar offered wide open spaces and fresh air along with an easy train ride to Albany to work or to shop.

In those first few decades of the twentieth century, teachers were tasked with instructing their students in the subjects of reading, writing, spelling, geography, and arithmetic; there was no such thing as physical education in the curriculum. Most schools also fielded a baseball team each spring and the teams would play games occasionally with nearby schools. This tradition extended at least through the 1960s.

In 1917, a new piece of legislation called the Township School Bill was proposed by Governor Whitman. It was seen as revolutionary for that time as the law provided for the ability of towns to centralize the schools within their borders so only one board of trustees would be necessary instead of the common school tradition of a board of trustees for each common school. This legislation also allowed for a specialized high school curriculum to be developed, taught, and made available to students within an entire county. Such a school existed in Delmar during the 1917–18 school year.

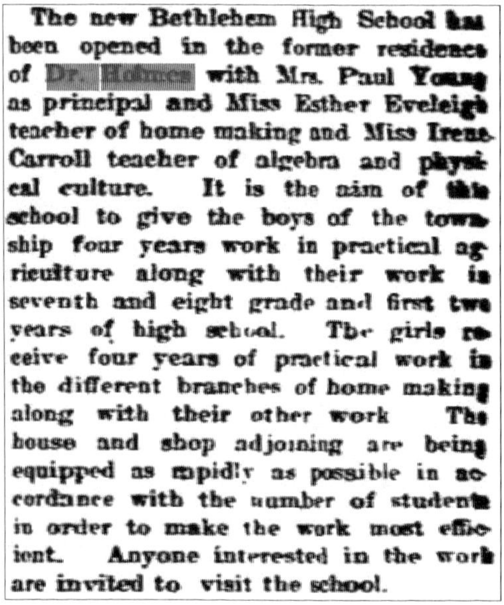

> The new Bethlehem High School has been opened in the former residence of Dr. [illegible] with Mrs. Paul Young as principal and Miss Esther Eveleigh teacher of home making and Miss Irene Carroll teacher of algebra and physical culture. It is the aim of this school to give the boys of the township four years work in practical agriculture along with their work in seventh and eight grade and first two years of high school. The girls receive four years of practical work in the different branches of home making along with their other work. The house and shop adjoining are being equipped as rapidly as possible in accordance with the number of students in order to make the work most efficient. Anyone interested in the work are invited to visit the school.

FIGURE 2-4 Clipping describing the experimental high school in Delmar, 21 September 1917 (courtesy *Altamont Enterprise*)

This new school program was an experimental high school curriculum, based on a national push for farmers to have access to the best methods of scientific farming. The result, it was hoped, would be increased farm production and raised awareness for the public about the profits of farming. The school was the only one of its type in Albany County, and children in the Town of Bethlehem could attend for free. Any other child wishing to attend from within Albany County paid a small tuition fee (Figure 2-4).

There was concern about children not being able to take traditional school classes, so the curriculum was combined in a way that made it possible for children to study traditional core subjects such as reading, writing, spelling, geography, and arithmetic in addition to agriculture, domestic science (for the young ladies), and mechanical arts. The idea was to integrate the new courses into the current seventh and eighth grade curriculums and then create two further years of study that would mimic the first two years of high school. The use of a private home owned by Dr. Thomas Holmes, who was serving in World War I, was set aside as the base of operations.

However, though the school was deemed a rousing success, the experimental high school lasted only one year. It was created as a result of the passage of the Township School Act, signed into law by Governor Whitman. In the winter of 1918, however, the legislature repealed the Act, and funding for the school was no longer available. Sadly, no school board minutes exist from this time as the clerk never fulfilled his job requirement. What little is known has been gleaned from newspaper articles. There would not be another high school until 1926.

Though the 1920 Federal Census shows only a marginal increase in population (less than 1 percent), more children were beginning to attend school regularly. School Board minutes in March 1922 show that over 180 students were in attendance in the Delmar School. Upwards of forty students, split into two grades, were inhabiting a single classroom. Often there was one teacher per classroom. The lower grades were the most populated, so at times an additional teacher was hired. With the building now bursting at the seams, a committee was appointed to determine if a new building was needed or if an addition would be suitable.

A member of the committee, Professsor Chase of the Albany Schools, reported for the committee that the present building was considered inadequate for the current school population. The committee proposed the addition of at least two classrooms. It is noted in the board minutes in March 1923 that a temporary two-room building was purchased at a cost of $3770 (payable over seven years). This building was a Quonset hut and housed the second and third grades.

However, the minutes also noted that while the overcrowding was temporarily relieved, the district would need to act to provide adequate school facilities for the future. It was deemed that a new building was the most prudent solution. Important to this recommendation were several reasons:

1. More than forty students per classroom is too many.
2. Expert students should not be detained in their studies when they can do higher-level work than the grade in which they started.

3. One classroom per grade level.
4. Pupils from outside the district would provide an annual income from the state of New York.
5. (Likely the most important reason) Albany High was overcrowded, and if they could not accept outside students that could be a problem.

Also important to the consideration of building a high school was to organize a Union Free School District. Remember, the town of Bethlehem was made up of many individual Common Schools. Designation as a Union Free School District (UFSD) would allow:
1. The ability to create and implement a high school curriculum.
2. A UFSD would pay for transportation of pupils living two miles, or further, from school.
3. More than one district could be part of the makeup of a UFSD. For example, several of the individual districts within the Town of Bethlehem could merge and form a UFSD.
4. A larger school could be used for community purposes.

By the early 1920s Frank Hungerford had established a bus line, thus creating the possibility for school bus transportation. In April 1924 public votes were taken to allow the construction of a new school and to create a UFSD; in addition, voters had to choose one of six possible sites identified by a committee as the location of the new school. The possible sites were as follows:
1. The Woods site
2. The Rowe farm
3. A combination Woods-Rowe site
4. The Bennett farm site
5. The Borthwick site
6. The library site.

Voting resulted in the Borthwick site being chosen as the first option (158) with the library site coming in second (144). The committee voted to spend $500 to have both sites surveyed to determine draining, filling, and grading needs.

By August of 1924, the question of the site was settled. The Borthwick Avenue site was chosen by a vote of 301 in favor, 205 against.

FIGURE 2-5 Newspaper photo of the town's first high school, Delmar High, under construction at the corner of Borthwick and Delaware Avenues. Built on property that functioned as the town baseball field. The building is now the Town Hall (courtesy the *Albany Times Union*).

However, in an August 1, 1924, article in the *Altamont Enterprise* the proponents of the library site vowed the "fight for the control of education in the school district would be carried into the fall primaries and election in a final effort to defeat the present Board of Education." It is unknown if this was carried out.

The property at the corner of Delaware and Borthwick Avenues was purchased for $15,000. The State Education Department approved the site and town voters gave their approval to the cost (approximately $172,000) of the new school. One of the concerns of the State Education Department was the lack of "physical training." There was no place in the curriculum for the students to experience physical activity during the day. This was another area to be addressed by the new school. Building plans included a gymnasium that would also serve as an auditorium (Figure 2-5).

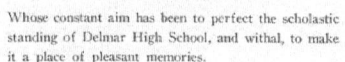

FIGURE 2-6 (LEFT) Mr. Olin Bouck, in the first issue of Delmar High's yearbook, the Oriole, in 1929 (courtesy *Oriole* yearbook).

FIGURE 2-7 (RIGHT) Mr. Heth Coons, who served as principal at the high school's original site and at its Kenwood Avenue site (courtesy *Oriole* yearbook, 1938)

In preparation for development of a high school curriculum, it became obvious a well-qualified high school teacher was needed. Mr. Olin Bouck (Figure 2-6) was hired prior to the 1925–26 school year. Bouck taught at Delmar School (Masonic Temple site) for that school year and in 1926 assumed the job of principal of the new Delmar High at a salary of $1,000 per year. Mr. Bouck was instrumental in the development of Delmar High School, as was another educator named Mr. Heth Coons (Figure 2-7).

Delmar High retained its name for only six years. Centralization of schools happened in 1930 when Bethlehem Central was formed. The 1934 school yearbook is the first to sport the Bethlehem Central High school name. In subsequent decades, the original high school building at the corner of Delaware and Borthwick Avenues became Delmar Elementary School. The Masons purchased the original Delmar School building at the corner of Kenwood Avenue and Adams Street. Those classrooms would be pressed into service at various times over the years as the district expanded and reconfigured.

Due to declining enrollments, Delmar Elementary closed in June 1976. The building went through a period of refurbishment and reopened as the Bethlehem Town Hall in 1980. As an elementary school, it was much loved by its students and their parents. It is impossible to name all of the memorable teachers, but the following names (in no particular order) cropped up most frequently during interviews of former students: Allen, Hosey, Gunther, Crysler, Williams, Cronin, Oliver, Smith, and its longest tenured principal, Mr. George Bonacker.

Mr. Bonacker presided over Delmar School from 1946 to 1971. According to notes kept by Mrs. Dorothy Hosey (a 41-year veteran teacher) for the district's 50th Anniversary Celebration, "Mr. George F. Bonacker was a young, vigorous, personable man with a great drive and insatiable desire to improve our school." Mr. Bonacker was quick to realize that the building was built for high school students and some remodeling was needed to provide a safer environment for the smaller children.

Bonacker arrived on the tails of a "short-term" principal; his appointment followed the untimely death, from a heart attack, of Mr. Arlington F. Smith (Figure 2-8), a much-loved administrator who had recently transferred to Delmar School from a nine-year tenure as principal of Elsmere School.

Mr. Smith arrived in Bethlehem in 1931 upon being hired as the principal of Elsmere School. After nine years at Elsmere, he assumed the principalship of Delmar School, where he provided a framework that, according to Mrs. Dorothy Hosey, allowed "programs designed to teach formalized education combined with creativeness to a more 'middle of the road' approach to educating the youth of our time. Self-discipline, self-worth, and self-esteem went hand in hand with productivity and high standards to work to your ability to mold the students." This seems to have resulted in, again according to Mrs. Dorothy Hosey, the

SCHOOLS HONOR LATE PRINCIPAL

Officials and teachers in the Bethlehem Central school district, former students and present pupils in Delmar grade school will pay final tribute to Principal Arlington F. Smith at funeral services Friday at 11 a. m. at the Applebee Funeral home, 403 Delaware avenue, Delmar. The Rev. LeRoy C. Brandt, pastor of Delmar Reformed church, will officiate and burial will be at Addison.

Mr. Smith, 40, principal of the Delmar school since September, 1942, died Tuesday night in Albany hospital after a few days illness.

Born at Addison, son of the late Frank and Maude Smith, he started his teaching career in rural schools in Steuben county in 1924. Later he taught at Smithtown, L. I., rural schools of Montgomery county and Troy High school, before moving to Delmar in 1931.

1931-1942 AT ELSMERE

He served as principal of Elsmere grade school from 1931 until 1942, when he transferred to the Delmar school.

A brief memorial service in honor of Principal Smith was conducted at a special assembly in Delmar school yesterday afternoon by the Rev. Dr. Brandt.

Principal Smith was a graduate of State College for Teachers with the class of 1936 and did post-graduate work at teachers' college of Columbia university, and at New York university.

Because of his death, the dance which was to have been conducted tomorrow night at Delmar school under auspices of the Parent-Teacher association has been postponed.

Hamilton H. Bookhout, supervising principal of the Bethlehem Central School district, announced last night that all schools in the district will be closed Friday afternoon as a mark of respect to Principal Smith.

FIGURE 2-8 Mr. Arlington F. Smith obituary (courtesy the *Albany Times Union*).

Delmar School of the late 1930s and early 1940s having a curriculum that was of the "do as you please if you're interested" philosophy.

(Because Mrs. Hosey taught at the Delmar School from 1942 to 1975, her thoughts are integral to its history.)

Unfortunately, Mr. Smith had been principal at Delmar for just over two years when he passed away on September 19, 1944. Because he had been in Bethlehem since 1931, and each school community is a microcosm of the community surrounding it, the reaction of the Delmar community was great in its scope. All of the schools in the district closed on September 22, 1944 so his service at the Applebee Funeral Home could be attended by the many who wished to pay their respects.

FIGURE 2-9 Mr. Dean Allen (courtesy *Oriole* yearbook, 1959).

Arlington Smith left a widow—Florence, or Flossie as she was known—and a son, Lauren. Mrs. Flossie Smith worked as an elementary teacher and librarian in the district from 1931 to 1971.

Another longtime teacher at Delmar School was Mrs. Florence Allen. She taught at the school for almost twenty years, mostly first grade. Widowed in 1947, she was left to raise her only child, Dean. By all accounts Dean Brooks Allen grew up to be a fine young man. An accomplished diver, Dean earned a scholarship to Indiana University after his graduation in 1959 from BCHS. Many former students and classmates recalled Dean's prowess in the pool, and he was a popular swimming instructor within the town (Figure 2-9).

FIGURE 2-10 Lt. Dean Allen, featured in Andrew Carroll's book, *War Letters: Extraordinary Letters from American Wars* (courtesy https://www.aarp.org/home-family/friends-family/info-2014/soldiers-last-letters-home.html).

Dean was eventually drafted into the U.S. Army during the Vietnam War. He chose to attend Officer Candidate School. Dean's last letter home to his wife, Joyce, is one of many featured in Andrew Carroll's book *War Letters*. In the letter Dean tells his wife, "Maybe sometime I'll even try to tell you how scared I have been or am now. Sometimes I really wonder how I'll make it. My luck is running way [to] good right now. I just hope it lasts." Four days later, on July 15, 1969, Dean stepped on a land mine while leading a search-and-destroy mission in Binh Long Province. He succumbed to his injuries on July 18, 1969. A brief article in the July 30, 1969, issue of the *Albany Times Union* describes his passing, along with plans for his funeral service, with full military honors, at Applebee Funeral Home (Figure 2-10).

Dean's loss was certainly not the only one among Bethlehem's boys. Perhaps it is magnified in memory by his character and the fact his mother was a longtime member of the school community (Figure 2-11).

FIGURE 2-11 One of Mrs. Florence Allen's first grade classes, many of whom graduated in 1976 (courtesy Sally Knox Sakshaug '76).

FIGURE 2-12 Mr. and Mrs. Vernon Oliver (courtesy Richard Owen '63).

Another Delmar School alumnus spoke of how he had been in Mr. Vernon Oliver's last sixth grade class. That was a mysterious comment. The former student revealed Mr. Oliver died during the summer of 1957, and he even sent a photograph of Mr. Vernon Oliver and his wife. They stand confidently in the photograph. Subsequent research revealed an article from the *Plattsburgh Press-Republican* describing the accident that befell Mr. Oliver. Mr. Oliver and his wife were in a small rowboat on Lake Champlain near Willsboro Point. Both were from that area. The couple decided to trade places in the boat, and, during that exchange, the boat capsized in seven feet of water. A good swimmer, Mr. Oliver struck his head during the fall and was rendered unconscious. His wife was unable to get him to shore (Figure 2-12).

LONG DEAD, HE LIVES—Mrs. Dorothy Hosey joins in a moment of silent meditation with her Delmar Elementary School Fourth Grade Class over the grave of Spanish American War veteran Cpl. Richard Hogan. The soldier, whose grave has been long neglected, lives on in the memory of the school children who paid tribute to him at St. Agnes' Cemetery in Menands. (Times-Union Photo by Fred McKinney)

FIGURE 2-13 Mrs. Dorothy Hosey and class (courtesy *Albany Times Union*).

By all accounts, Mr. Oliver was a well-liked teacher by students and parents alike. He was a decorated veteran of the Korean War. Newspaper articles from the time show he was active as a faculty representative within the community. Incidents such as these stick in the minds of impressionable young students. Thankfully, they are overshadowed by happier events and experiences.

Another faculty fixture at Delmar School was Mrs. Dorothy Hosey. She was well known for class field trips and widespread involvement with local politicians, notably Congressmen Leo O'Brien and Samuel Stratton. In fact, Mrs. Hosey worked with her fourth-grade classes to propose a permanent holiday in honor of assassinated President John F. Kennedy. Though she pursued this effort well past her retirement, it never came to fruition (Figure 2-13).

Discussions among former students regarding Mrs. Hosey were polarized. She was remembered fondly or not so fondly, in equal numbers. An amusing anecdote passed along by a circa 1950 Delmar School student related Mrs. Hosey's penchant for sending this student on personal errands during the school day. The former student clearly remembers being sent to the Delmar Department Store, at the Four Corners, to purchase a slip for Mrs. Hosey. Mrs. Hosey was well-known for being "dressed to the nines" for school each day.

Other Delmar School students recalled being sent by teachers to Jasper's corner store, just across the street on the other corner of Delaware and Borthwick Avenues. This event involved buying candy for the class. One girl was sent to Jasper's to buy full-size Tootsie Rolls for Mrs. Gunther's entire third-grade class. That would not happen today!

Delmar School memories also include trips to the New York State Museum, in its former Washington Avenue location in the State Education Building, to view the numerous dioramas of Iroquois culture along with the giant mastodon. Students also went to the Delmar Game Farm (now Five Rivers) and walked down the street to the Delmar Fire House. Popular teacher Mrs. Oliver brought items from Japan, where she had taught previously, to enhance learning for children. And Mr. Hugh Williams greatly expanded outdoor education curriculum begun by Dr. Ron Bover of Clarksville School (Figure 2-14) and regularly took his classes on innovative outdoor trips to nearby Lawson's Lake. This initial push for environmental learning secured itself into children's experiences for decades and is

FIGURE 2-14 Dr. Ron Bover (courtesy *Syracuse Post-Star*).

FIGURE 2-15 Mr. Hugh Williams (courtesy *Albany Times Union*).

still included in different forms in the district-wide fifth grade experience (Figures 2-15, 2-16).

Though there is much more to the Delmar School story, this provides a snippet of the importance of this original school. It may be said that Delmar School was the foundation of the school district. Elsmere School construction followed a few years later. These two schools were anchors in the community, aided by their centralized locations. Each school was often the site of a whole host of community meetings, concerts, and dances until the larger school on Kenwood Avenue (the present-day middle school) was built in the mid-1930s.

FIGURE 2-16 (RIGHT) Lawson Lake Patch (courtesy Laurie Holder Meyer '76).

The much-loved Delmar School closed its doors permanently at the end of the 1975-76 school year. Overall enrollment within the district was declining, the school was in disrepair, and students could be divided up between the other elementary schools. A deal was struck between the district and the town and after renovations, the school reopened as the Bethlehem Town Hall in 1980. Any former student who had the misfortune to appear in Town Court may have remembered the many peanut butter and jelly sandwiches consumed in the former school cafeteria-turned-courtroom.

FIGURE 2-17 Mr. George Bonacker, longtime Delmar School principal (Courtesy Beth Anderson '76)

FIGURE 3-1 Original Elsmere School, District No. 15 (courtesy Town of Bethlehem).

FIGURE 3-2 Elsmere School class with Mrs. Mettie Sexton standing in the center of the back row (courtesy Town of Bethlehem).

CHAPTER 3

ELSMERE SCHOOL

ELSMERE SCHOOL (Figure 3-1) was the last of the one-room schoolhouses to be built in the town of Bethlehem. The original school building was located on Elsmere Avenue where the old Legion Hall stood (in those days, the roadbed was level with the railroad tracks). Known as District #15, the Elsmere school operated from 1911 to 1929, with the original school building being replaced by a new building at a different location in 1928. Its first principal was Mrs. Mettie E. Sexton (Figure 3-2), who, according to local longtime resident and teacher Mr. Al Restifo (Figure 3-3), had been teaching children in her home on Elsmere Avenue as early as 1904. Her home, which no longer stands, was located in what is now part of the St. Stephen's Church parking lot.

Prior to 1910, students from Elsmere had attended the District #11 (Normansville) school, which stood on the hill to the left of the current Delaware Avenue just prior to going over the Normanskill Bridge. The site is currently occupied by a small, multi-use office building.

The railroad played a tremendously important role in the development of the Tri-Village area. It brought farm goods, notably milk,

FIGURE 3-3 Mr. Alfred Restifo '45, Elsmere School alumnus and longtime teacher at Clarksville and the Middle School (courtesy *Albany Times Union*).

FIGURE 3-4 The new Elsmere School (courtesy Town of Bethlehem).

to the market, it brought people to and from school and work, and it brought teachers to their schools. Several former students recalled the thrill of greeting a teacher at the railroad station each day and escorting her to the school building. In the case of the early Elsmere School, this was an easy task because the school building was so close to the railroad tracks.

The new Elsmere School was built in 1927 at the corner of Delaware and Herrick Avenues, and opened for students in 1928, not long after Delmar High opened on the corner of Delaware and Borthwick Avenues. Herrick Avenue was instrumental in guiding people to a lovely assortment of houses in a growing neighborhood.

The school boasted six classrooms, one each for grades 1 through 6, as well as a gymnasium. During the 1920s there was a nationwide push to showcase the importance of physical education and to include it as a required curriculum element. It coincided with the push for people to move to the suburbs because it was a cleaner environment and allowed for fresh air and space for children to play. To accommodate the ever-increasing district enrollment in the 1930s, many high school dances were held in the new Elsmere gym while a larger school was being built for grades 7 through 12.

The Elsmere School building has had several additions and changes over the past several decades: in 1948, it received a library and seven additional classrooms; in 1964 it received an addition consisting of three classrooms, a kitchen, a cafeteria, and locker room/shower facilities. As the building continues to be used as a school, additions and changes continue to this day.

Each elementary school had a string of beloved principals. When Elsmere School opened its doors at the Delaware Avenue location in 1928, it was with a male principal at the helm. It was stipulated that the principal position "was to be held by a man," according to an article in the *Altamont Enterprise*. The principal would receive a salary of $1,900 a year. In 1931, Mr. Arlington Smith was hired as principal; in addition to this, he also taught sixth grade (his initial salary was $2,000—roughly $35,000 in today's dollars—but he reimbursed the school $100 at the end of the year to equalize salaries; while this was not an outstanding salary, it must be remembered that the country was entering an economic depression at that time). Arlington Smith's wife, Mrs. Florence (Flossie) Smith, also taught in the school district for over 35 years, 17 of them as a school librarian. Another longtime principal at Elsmere was Mr. Richard Herrmann; his wife, Mrs. Jeanne Herrmann, was a teacher at Delmar School for many years and a familiar sight on her bicycle as she pedaled to and from school.

Given the busy nature of the present-day Delaware Avenue, it is difficult to imagine it as a dusty two-lane thoroughfare with the utility poles immediately adjacent to the side of the road. Plus, it was a bit more residential in the past, with a mix of stately homes interspersed with a smattering of bungalows. Businesses were not as abundant as they are now (Figure 3-5).

FIGURE 3-5 Older Delaware Avenue, corner of Elsmere Avenue (courtesy Town of Bethlehem).

On the school's 75th anniversary in late 2002, many former students wrote letters to then principal Dorothy Whitney about their time at Elsmere School. One former student, a retired college professor, wrote that he was in the first class at the new Elsmere School in 1928. Among his two distinct memories were 1) being recognized in the third grade for writing the best composition—he went on to become an accomplished writer and professor—and 2) though he did not remember in what grade level it took place, the sudden death of his first girlfriend—a girl named Kathy—from a childhood disease. This experience left a lasting impression—"his first love; his first death."

Another Elsmere student recalled having difficulty learning division. The principal dropped by the classroom and took the student to the chalkboard where the principal "patiently" showed the student how to do the division. "This gave me the boost I needed," shared the former student. The principal mentioned in this anecdote was Mr. Richard Herrmann, who served as principal of Elsmere School from 1952 to 1984. (3-6)

Another former classmate told of one particular autumn when students were taken to the auditorium each day to watch the World

FIGURE 3-6 Elsmere sign (courtesy Wikimedia Commons).

Series on television. According to this student, the contest between the New York Yankees and the Brooklyn Dodgers was memorable to her "because we did not have a television at home." This same student also noted in her letter that milk was sold in small glass bottles and students used narrow paper straws to drink the milk. Her sandwich, from home, was always wrapped in an old bread bag that crinkled and made lots of noise when she opened it. She envied her girlfriends whose sandwiches were wrapped in "Cutrite" wax paper bags (Figure 3-7). Several former students remembered stopping at a local gas station on their walks home from school to share a soda; it was a treat to sip an ice-cold bottle of soda from a machine in those days. Many tales of play were shared, as the area surrounding the Elsmere School neighborhood was rife with ravines and creeks.

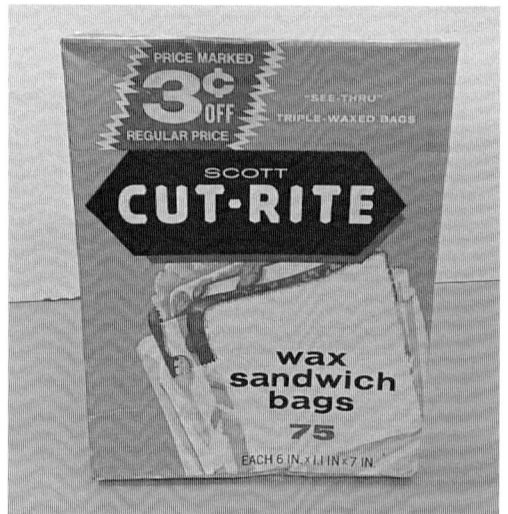

FIGURE 3-7 Cut-Rite wax paper sandwich bags (courtesy eBay.com).

Just as each elementary school had its distinct neighborhoods, each school had its own gathering place for students to buy candy and treats. For Elsmere schoolchildren, this was Barracini's, a small store located in a white house near the railroad tracks. The house still stands on the right just past the railroad underpass on Elsmere Avenue.

Elsmere School was important to the community; this is exemplified by dozens of articles in the *Altamont Enterprise* in which the school is mentioned. Scout troops met there, plays were performed, dances were held, and concerts were given. Though these events date back to the late 1920s, the same holds true today.

One former Elsmere student (BCHS '44) related that she loved the school and its neighborhood. At the time she entered elementary school,

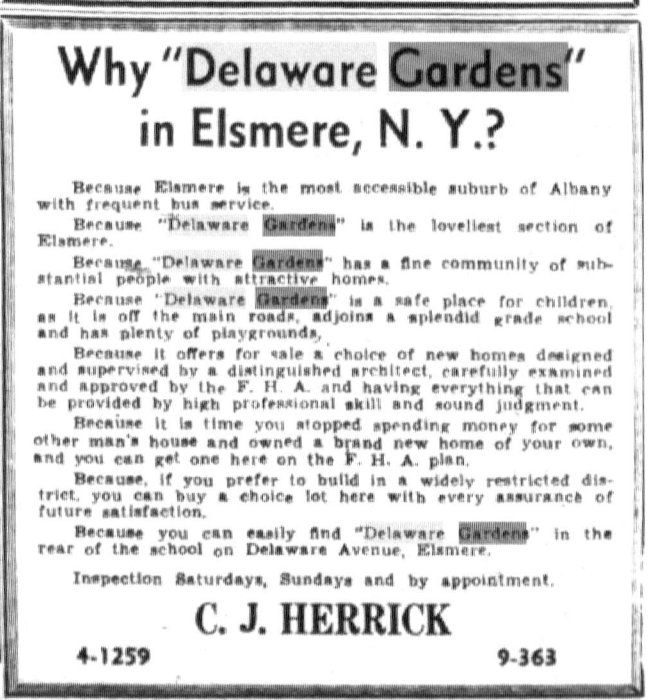

FIGURE 3-8 Delaware Gardens real estate advertisement (courtesy *Albany Times Union*).

her family moved to "Delaware Gardens," a newly built housing development adjacent to, and behind, the Elsmere School (Figure 3-8). The family's residence was on Herrick Avenue and is still there today. She loved the fact that there was so much "wild territory" in which to play.

What is at once charming, and amusing, is the name of the subdivision—Delaware Gardens. Lost in our present-day population is the naming of these neighborhoods. The names were designed to foster the image of the cleanliness of the suburbs…free from the congestion and germs of the city.

Students over the years have wondered about teachers' lives outside of the school building. They were amazed to learn that their beloved teachers were regular people. In the early years of the school district, after centralization, teachers were required to live within the Town of Bethlehem. Therefore, they were integral parts of many neighborhoods. One former Elsmere student recalled that Mrs. Etta Cass, one of the early Elsmere principals, lived at the corner of Delaware Avenue and Rural Place. He also noted that another principal, Mr. Arlington Smith, lived on Lincoln Avenue in Elsmere. We already know the original principal, Mrs. Mettie Sexton, lived on Elsmere Avenue.

It is enjoyable to read the recollections of the former students. Very often the memories are told from their childhood perspectives, which are unadulterated and refreshing, if sometimes wistful. One man recollected he and a classmate got an afternoon off in the third grade. He had to take his young friend home because the end of the friend's bandaged finger had come off. As the individual wrote, "Apparently 'old Doc Browne' did not get it reattached as well as he should have." The same two childhood friends also told of being "in love" with their respective sixth-grade teachers. Both teachers lived in an apartment in the same house where Drs. Gainor and Giombetti practiced medicine.

These are several snapshots of life at Elsmere School in its first fifty years of existence. As it approaches its 100th anniversary, it will be fascinating to hear of more recent memories (Figure 3-9).

FIGURE 3-9 Elsmere's 1925 eighth grade graduating class, the last in the original District No. 15 school (courtesy Town of Bethlehem).

FIGURE 4-1 1866 map (courtesy Old-Maps.com).

CHAPTER 4

CLARKSVILLE SCHOOL

THE CLARKSVILLE COMMUNITY has most closely retained the rural roots that pervaded many settlements surrounding the city of Albany. The hamlet of Clarksville is located about fifteen miles southwest of the city of Albany. Due to its location on the former Bethlehem Turnpike (now NYS route 443), it quickly became a popular resting stop for people traveling from Albany to Berne, Rensselaerville, and beyond. Ironically, though the hamlet is in the Town of New Scotland, its school became part of the Bethlehem Central School District (Figure 4-1).

A school was present in the hamlet as early as 1775, and residents were primarily engaged in dairy farming and lime-burning. In 1825, the original log schoolhouse was replaced by one of stone. As the 1800s progressed, public education became compulsory throughout the United States and New York State passed legislation leading to education reforms right about 1880. Due to the state's recommendations for the construction of the common schools (one-room schoolhouses), the stone school built in 1825 was torn down and a new one built in its place. The "new" school utilized the stones from the former school in its foundation and was constructed for $600.00 (roughly $11,000–$12,000 today). This school building was modified over the decades from one room to two rooms, back to one room, and then to two rooms.

In its early days, Clarksville School was District #2 of the sixteen individual school districts within the Town of New Scotland. Bethlehem had a total of fifteen. In the latter part of the 1800s District

FIGURE 4-2 Students at the old school in 1913 (courtesy Town of Bethlehem).

#2 contained the largest number of school-age children (Figure 4-2). Approximately 75 percent of the eligible children attended school. During the first third of the twentieth century, educational reformers determined that the common school system was becoming obsolete. The reformers pushed for centralization of schools. The Town of New Scotland disassembled its school district, and the schools were absorbed by neighboring school districts.

An *Altamont Enterprise* article from December 1926 lists students at Clarksville School who made the Honor Roll and attained perfect attendance for the previous month. Of the ten Honor Roll students, four are later found as graduates in the *Oriole* Yearbook. It is not clear how students were able to travel to Delmar to attend high school. Students living in Voorheesville were able to easily access the local train. While some bus lines were established as early as 1918, it is unknown if any traveled to Clarksville.

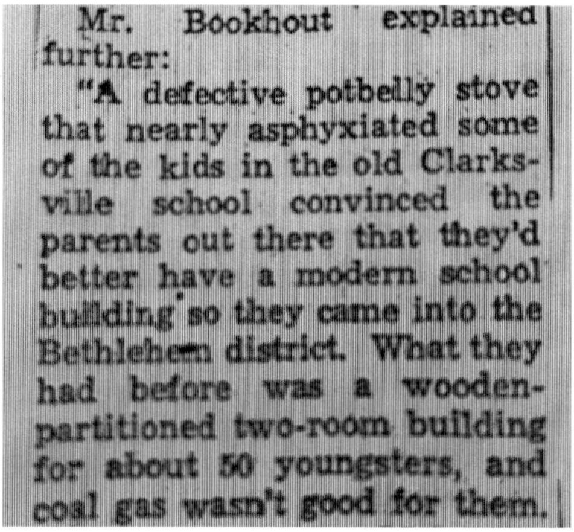

> Mr. Bookhout explained further:
> "A defective potbelly stove that nearly asphyxiated some of the kids in the old Clarksville school convinced the parents out there that they'd better have a modern school building so they came into the Bethlehem district. What they had before was a wooden-partitioned two-room building for about 50 youngsters, and coal gas wasn't good for them.

FIGURE 4-3 Snippet from *Times Union* article mentioning a defective coal stove (courtesy *Albany Times Union*).

As farming decreased in the towns of New Scotland and Bethlehem, and the towns moved from being rural to suburban, more families moved into the areas. By the early 1940s the Clarksville School had again expanded to two rooms. A story in the March 5, 1942 *Times Union* reports that students were sent home from the Clarksville School due to the odor of coal gas. In a story printed two days later, Mr. Olin Bouck, the Bethlehem district superintendent, claimed the school was never closed and the gas leak had been repaired. There is a discrepancy in that one story reported the principal of the school was to send children home if there was any odor of gas. And yet, Mr. Bouck claimed the school was never closed. Also, at least one newspaper article reported that two children had been overcome with symptoms and another reported no consequences due to the gas leaks (Figure 4-3). At the very least, the residents of Clarksville became aware of the need for an improved school facility. The school was closed, and the students were divided and sent to schools in Bethlehem and Voorheesville.

However, by the mid-1940s Voorheesville, in the Town of New Scotland—which would have been the closest area to Clarksville—did not have the revenue stream to build a new school. Therefore, the Clarksville community decided to join the Bethlehem Central School District (BCSD). Population had been increasing steadily in the Town of Bethlehem since the late 1920s and the BCSD could count on the revenue stream needed to sustain a school in Clarksville, so they promised to build one if Clarksville voted to join the BCSD.

An article from the *Times Union* in November of 1945 reports that the Bethlehem Central Board of Education granted permission for additions to both Elsmere School and the High School. Also, the Board of Education granted permission to build a new elementary school in Clarksville. Citizens of the Town of Bethlehem and in Clarksville voted to fund the proposed additions and new construction. Also of note is the news of a 16-acre tract of land purchased in the Hamagrael section of Delmar for future use. Just two years later, the paper reported that the existing Clarksville School was wholly inadequate. Of the 128 school-age elementary students, 72 were being taught at the Clarksville School and 56 (fifth and sixth graders) were either at Delmar or Slingerlands Schools. In addition, the Clarksville School had recently been damaged by fire (Figure 4-4).

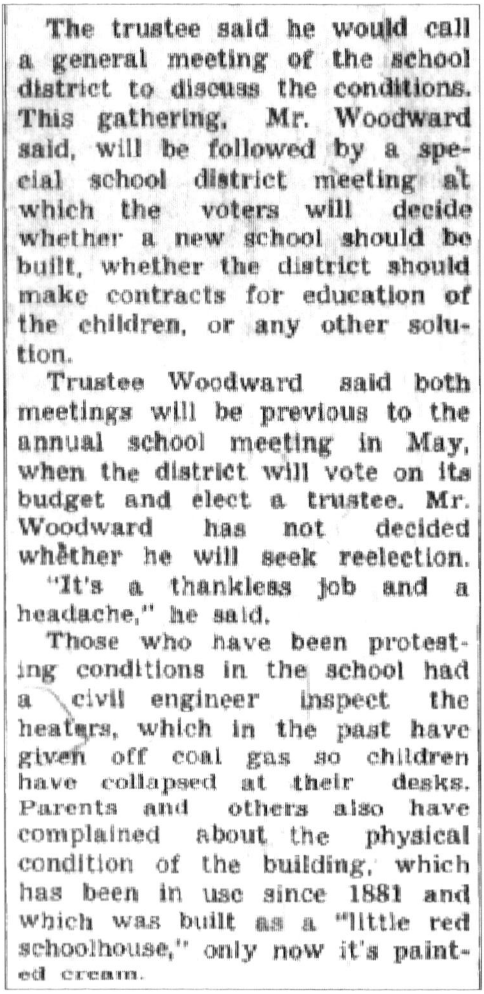

> The trustee said he would call a general meeting of the school district to discuss the conditions. This gathering, Mr. Woodward said, will be followed by a special school district meeting at which the voters will decide whether a new school should be built, whether the district should make contracts for education of the children, or any other solution.
>
> Trustee Woodward said both meetings will be previous to the annual school meeting in May, when the district will vote on its budget and elect a trustee. Mr. Woodward has not decided whether he will seek reelection.
>
> "It's a thankless job and a headache," he said.
>
> Those who have been protesting conditions in the school had a civil engineer inspect the heaters, which in the past have given off coal gas so children have collapsed at their desks. Parents and others also have complained about the physical condition of the building, which has been in use since 1881 and which was built as a "little red schoolhouse," only now it's painted cream.

FIGURE 4-4 Discussion of new school as reported in *The Albany County Post* (courtesy *The Albany County Post*).

Land for a new school was purchased in 1946 from Mr. George Teeling at a cost of $1,450. Mr. Teeling, a professional heating engineer, was a new member of the School Board. He was able to sell the Board on his plan to provide a modern school for the Clarksville area. An architect named Mr. Henry Blatner was hired for the project. Mr. Blatner, a District resident, had never designed a public building but was extremely interested in applying techniques from lighting research he had studied at MIT through his graduate work.

FIGURE 4-5 Former Woodside School (courtesy Susan Dee. Photo credit: Van or Jim LaGrange).

Mr. Blatner's plan was to incorporate the functionality of the one-floor rectangular design based on the influence of the Modern Movement, which would make it easy to expand if necessary. This newer movement in architecture advocated broad use of glass, steel, and concrete. The Board praised Blatner's modern design and undertook a professional advertising campaign to sell the plans to the residents. The school board members also carried out an unorthodox practice of

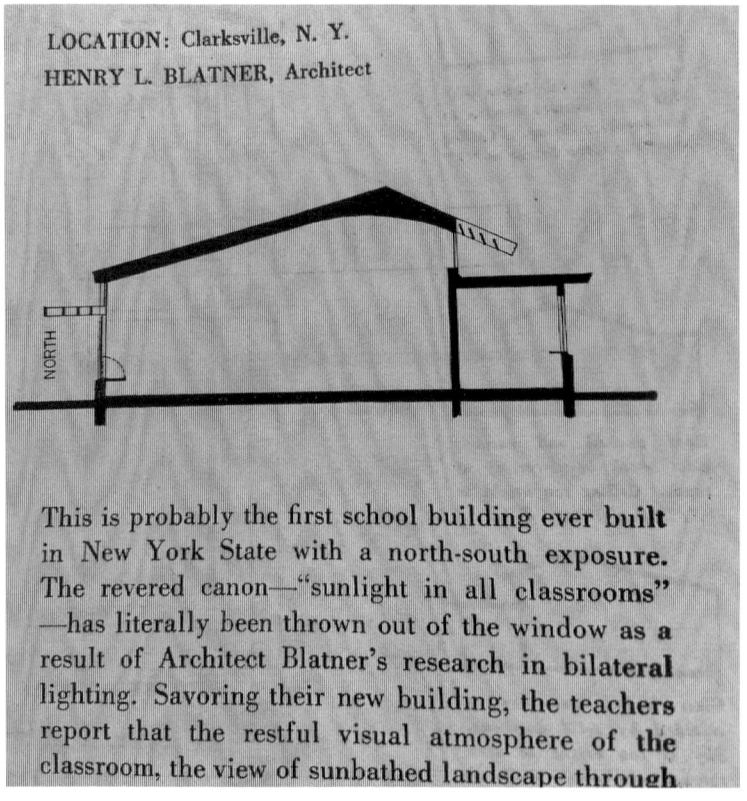

FIGURE 4-6 Beginning of journal article about Clarksville School design (courtesy *Architectural Forum*, October 1949).

campaigning in bars. Their argument was "You'll drink away tonight what the new schools will cost you [per] year." Statistical reinforcement for this argument was solid. At the time, the nation was spending an average of 1.5 percent of income on public schools and 6 percent for liquor and tobacco.

The bond issue passed overwhelmingly. Taxpayers assumed an average increase of $10 per year for the new school. Mr. Hamilton Bookhout, supervising principal of the Bethlehem Central district, noted, "We are sold on the small community for small children." In September 1948, at a cost of $210,000, the new Clarksville School opened. It incorporated the former one (or two)-room Town of New Scotland schoolhouses of Onesquethaw, Unionville, Stony Hill, and Woodside,

FIGURE 4-7 Design elements (courtesy *Architectural Forum*).

along with the original Clarksville School (Figure 4-5). Mrs. Frances Long moved to the new school from the Unionville location. She was remembered by many students over the years for such things as having taught the boys how to knit, being a known hair puller, and not being bothered by propriety when it came to pulling boys out of the rest room. Once a male student was liberated from the bathroom, she would exclaim, "I always get my man."

Due to the progressive thinking of the School Board, Mr. Blatner was allowed a great deal of latitude in the design of the school. Safety and sanitary regulations were a huge consideration in the design of a school building. To that end, the exterior of the buildings was often utilitarian and comprised of brick. Studies done at that time indicated a square classroom shape was more conducive to accommodating the newer teaching techniques than a rectangular classroom. Additionally, poor lighting had been linked to eye defects in adults. Continuous banks of windows along the north side were utilized, along with upper banks of glass block that were shaded by louvers and a bank of trees. Therefore, there was a great deal of natural indirect lighting, which was intended to cut down glare and eyestrain. The school plan was so innovative that articles were featured in several architectural publications including *The Architectural Forum* (Figure 4-6). An additional article in the *Times Union* in 1950, the new Clarksville School's first year in operation, describes some of the innovations featured in *The Architectural Forum* article.

Mr. Blatner's rectangular building design utilizing a north-south exposure was a first in New York State. A total of six classrooms lined a corridor, each with a door directly to the outdoors. The north side of the classrooms featured a five-foot-high window strip. Windowsills in each classroom were lowered to match the size of the elementary children. To reduce glare, a tree screen was planted along that side of the building. A bank of louvers along the roof line could also be utilized to reduce glare from the natural light, especially when the ground was covered with snow (Figure 4-7).

The south side of the building featured a clerestory, which allowed natural light into the building. Clerestory windows are installed in a strip along the top of a high wall to allow light into a building, especially the north sun into a south-facing building. Specific colors of paint, such as coral, yellow, and light green, were used for better eye comfort. The chalkboards were green glass boards used with yellow chalk, as this had a better impact on children's eyes. Each classroom door had its own color to make it easily identifiable as well.

The success of the school's design was not just by chance. Mr. Blatner built scale models of five different designs. Each model classroom was built at a 1/5 scale. The models were tested under a variety of weather conditions for foot-candle and brightness readings. One refinement was to provide for window boxes on the interior of the classroom that had lids which could be raised to cut down on snow glare. Ultimately, the design of the school also allowed for the possibility of future expansion (Figure 4-8).

The Clarksville School was an important part of the community, as are most schools. In addition to the usual school functions, many community-oriented meetings and functions took place in the building. Not only was the school cutting-edge for its time, but it was also a setting for some inventive education practices. Mr. Ray Stephany be-

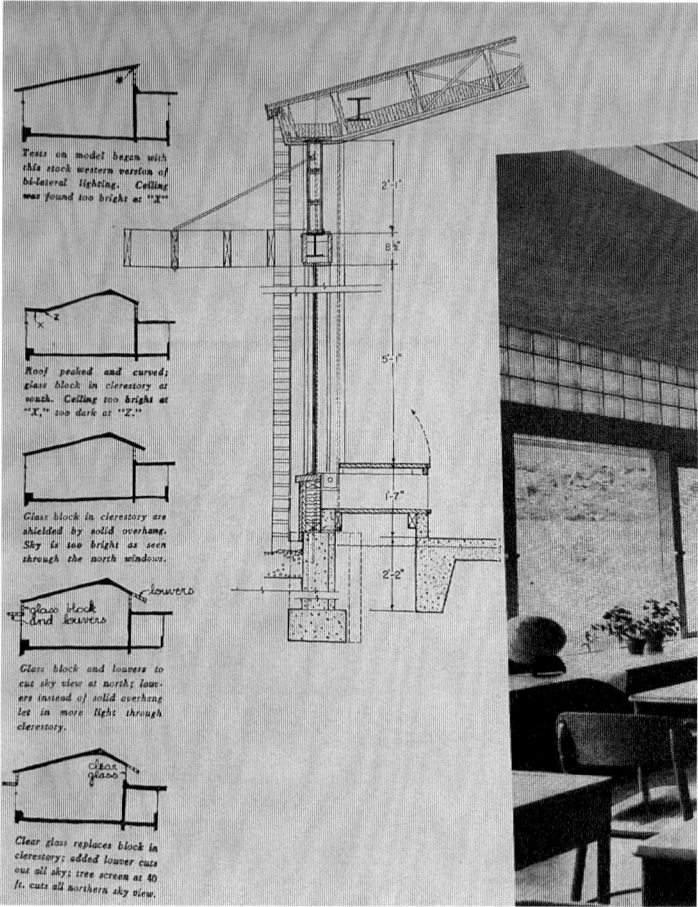

FIGURE 4-8 Lighting innovations (courtesy *Architectural Forum*).

came the principal of Clarksville in September of 1954. Along with a new principal, a new wing of the school containing a gymnasium, restrooms, a kitchen, the office, and the library opened at the same time. Under Mr. Stephany's guidance, the school was expanded twice more, the library doubled its resources, and a courtyard was added.

There were also some groundbreaking educational practices put into place. Mr. Stephany encouraged his faculty's creativity. He valued enrichment for his students. One teacher, Mr. Roland "Ron" Bover, initiated an outdoor education program at nearby Lawson's Lake in 1961. Though at least one other district teacher is most often associated with

FIGURE 4-9 Dr. Ron Bover (courtesy *Syracuse Post-Star*).

this program, Mr. Bover is the one who initiated it. Mr. Bover was also involved as an instructor in Heldeberg Workshop, and by the early 1970s he had left Clarksville to become the science supervisor and Outdoor Education director at the Campus-Community School at Cortland College in Cortland, New York (Figure 4-9).

Clarksville was the first school in the district to utilize an "Ungraded" program. A precursor to the "Open Classroom" program, the "Ungraded" program grouped students more by age and not by grade level. In the 1960s Clarksville received state funding to begin an experimental Pre-kindergarten program. This program provided a great deal of enriched preparation for students prior to beginning kindergarten. It was extraordinarily successful and ran for two years until state funding ran out. Despite its success, the district felt it was too expensive to continue. The school grew in leaps and bounds under Mr. Stephany's almost 20 years of leadership.

There were other principals over the years. These included Mr. Joe Schaefer, Mr. Dave Murphy, and Mrs. Dorothy Whitney, to name a few (Figure 4-10). Clarksville's last principal was one of its most beloved. Her name was Ms. Dorothy McDonald. Ms. McDonald was at the helm as the school-age population decreased in Clarksville and the difficult decision was reached by the Board to close the school in June of 2011 (Figure 4-11).

To know Ms. McDonald was to know how deeply she felt about children and teaching. Unfortunately, Dorothy became ill prior to Clarksville's last school year and passed away on September 28, 2010. The Superintendent paid tribute in his email to the parents of the Clarksville students by stating, "As she was away from Clarksville in recent

FIGURE 4-10 Sergeant Pat Dorsey and Mr. Dave Murphy overseeing bike safety at Clarksville School (courtesy Town of Bethlehem).

FIGURE 4-11 (LEFT) Ms. Dorothy McDonald (courtesy Bethlehem Central School District).

FIGURE 4-12 (RIGHT) One of Ms. Dorothy McDonald's pins (courtesy Ms. Heidi Bonacquist).

months, Ms. McDonald never stopped thinking about her students and their great adventures in learning. That's how she looked at school." Ms. McDonald was known for sporting a variety of pretty pins on her daily outfits. After her death, some of her colleagues and friends received a special gift from her family to remember her by (Figure 4-12).

And so, the school that Hamilton Bookhout fought to maintain because he believed in "decentralizing central schools," meaning he sought to have a network of neighborhood schools rather than transporting students all to one large school, went the way of centralized schools. Students would be taken to the new Eagle Elementary School, across from the high school, and to Slingerlands School.

Though the closure of the school affected the Clarksville community deeply, the property has come full circle in its use as a support of its neighborhood. The School District leased the site for several years to the Albany County Sheriff's Office for use as a satellite location. The Sheriff's Office had outgrown an office in Voorheesville and welcomed the opportunity to maintain a presence in Clarksville. The lease turned into a permanent sale, and to this day the Albany County Sheriff's continues to maintain their presence to aid the community.

FIGURE 5-1 Original Slingerlands Tollgate. Train tracks and printing business to the right (courtesy Town of Bethlehem).

FIGURE 5-2 The iconic Toll Gate Restaurant. Delicious homemade ice cream! (courtesy Town of Bethlehem).

CHAPTER 5

SLINGERLANDS SCHOOL

SLINGERLANDS, A HAMLET THAT GREW because of the actions of various members of the Slingerland family, began as a widespread settlement of working farms. It also benefited from the Albany–Rensselaerville Plank Road (now New Scotland Road), which ran through the area. Private companies were formed in the mid-1800s to improve the conditions of the roads. One method was to construct plank roads for ease of travel. To pay for the cost of construction and maintenance of these roads, tolls were collected at buildings known as tollgates (Figure 5-1). There were several tollgates within Bethlehem, including Slingerlands. These plank roads proved to be inadequate and were not utilized much past the 1860s. In the case of the Slingerlands hamlet, the term "tollgate" became memorable due to the Toll Gate Restaurant, which opened in 1949 and provided delicious ice cream until its closure in 2017 (Figure 5-2).

Slingerlands is split by its defunct railroad tracks, now part of the extensive Albany County Rail Trail. The railroad was especially important to the development of Slingerlands. The Delaware and Hudson Railroad, originally the Albany and Susquehanna, opened in 1863, providing travel to Albany and, by 1869, to Binghamton. Train travel through Delmar to Albany averaged 25 to 30 minutes (Figure 5-3).

Prior to the turn of the twentieth century, the hub of Slingerlands was the area north of the railroad tracks. Since that time, it has been on the South side of the railroad tracks where Kenwood Avenue meets New Scotland Road. It is interesting to note that a schoolhouse exist-

FIGURE 5-3 Slingerlands Train Station (courtesy Town of Bethlehem).

ed on the northern side until 1942, when the newer school opened on Union Avenue (part of the southern side).

Like the story of Delmar School, Slingerlands maintained its own schoolhouse well before 1900 and it was known as School District No. 9 (Figure 5-4). Town historian Susan Leath writes in her book *Images of America – Bethlehem*, "...this school building was torn down in 1908 and a new larger structure was built on the site." This second structure still stands on New Scotland Road, roughly across from the former Slingerlands Methodist Church, and was converted into apartments when the school on Union Avenue opened (Figure 5-5). Leath further tells us, "The last eighth grade graduated from here in 1931, with first through sixth grades continuing until 1946."

In an interview found in the Local History file at the Bethlehem Public Library, several women being interviewed about the Slingerlands Methodist Church in 1989 also provided some interesting information about the Slingerlands common school they attended. Mrs. Helen Earl Coughtry said there were no PTAs (Parent Teacher Associations) and there was one teacher upstairs in the school and one downstairs. She also recalled attending the small red-brick schoolhouse before it was replaced by the larger wood-frame building in 1908. After her grad-

FIGURE 5-4 Early Slingerlands school (courtesy Town of Bethlehem).

FIGURE 5-5 Second Slingerlands school, now an apartment building (courtesy Town of Bethlehem).

FIGURE 5-6 Slingerlands students at Albany High, 1915 (courtesy considerthesourceny.org).

uation in 1907 (eighth grade), she went, via train, to Albany High on Eagle Street in Albany. Another contemporary said she attended Milne (Figure 5-6).

The women also reported there were school tickets for the train that were cheaper for their parents to purchase. Mrs. Helen Coughtry and Mrs. Evelyn Frazier, whose father served one year as the school tax collector—each common school district had to support its own school—said that school taxes back then were $15 per year. At that time, the principal made $126 per month and the teachers took home $80–90 per month. Even considering that there were no paycheck deductions in those days, this was an insignificant amount of money. In 1908 an average factory worker made, on average, $200 per month.

FIGURE 5-7 1908 Slingerlands graduating class (courtesy Town of Bethlehem).

One influential teacher from those early years was Miss Boughton. She took the train to school each day from Albany. The women recalled she was very dedicated to preparing the students for the Regents exams at the end of their eighth-grade year. To graduate from the eighth grade, students had to pass the Regents with a grade of 75 percent or better (Figure 5-7). Most students took an exam in arithmetic, English, and history.

Taking the exams was nerve-wracking enough in itself for many students, but this was compounded by the fact that the students had to travel to Albany to take them. As one of the women said, "...and I didn't know anything more about Albany than I did Europe. I was so scared of getting lost."

The women recalled each school day began with a small prayer service and readings from the Bible. Singing also played a large part in the life of an elementary student. Students learned a wide variety of songs which helped them learn about life, friendship, God, country, and other countries as well. Other songs introduced additional languages to the young students. "Alouette" and "La Cucaracha" are two examples of these songs. Many of us are still able to recall songs learned in our youth at school. Of course, any songs of a religious nature are not allowed to be taught in public school today and there is no prayer of any sort.

History indicates a small brick structure once occupied the original school site across from the former Slingerlands Methodist Church on New Scotland Road. A 1908 article in the *Altamont Enterprise* decried the lack of sanitary conditions in the Slingerlands School. The decision was made to demolish the brick structure and to construct a larger wood-frame structure on the site. The two-story school building, which opened in 1909, still exists today as an apartment house. As roads continued to improve over the decades, the population of Slingerlands grew.

In 1938 the *Altamont Enterprise* reported a special election in the Town of Bethlehem. Voters approved a bond of $210,000, to which $176,000 of government funding was added. These monies were spent on additions to Elsmere School, the High School (present-day Middle School), and the construction of a new Slingerlands School.

In November 1941, students and teachers moved into the new brick school on Union Avenue. Almost 150 students were enrolled and enjoyed having a gymnasium that doubled as an auditorium. There were several classrooms, a dedicated kindergarten classroom, and an increased number of teachers (Figure 5-8). The principal then was Mr. James Smith. Mr. Smith, who also taught sixth grade, served in this role until he "was invited to join the Marines" in 1944. A local history file from the Bethlehem Public Library tells us that Mr. Smith continued to teach while in the Marines and eventually landed at Syracuse University in the Department of Teacher Education instead of returning to Slingerlands.

During the 1940s, the school had a few nicknames. Some called it "Ham Bookhout's Show Place." Apparently supervising principal Bookhout was immensely proud of his new school. He often visited the building, bringing others with him to view the school. Another nickname for the school was "Clyde Iron's Doll House." Mr. Clyde Irons was the much-loved custodian of the school. His care for the school was legendary. He knew every student by name and was on a first-name basis with the teachers. Mr. Irons took great pride in caring for the building.

While the school was new and had improved space and conditions, it lacked any sort of kitchen for lunch preparation. This was not unusual; in many schools, students brought their own lunches and some women from the community heated and served soup to any student

FIGURE 5-8 Slingerlands School 75th Anniversary celebration. Former teachers, from l. to r.: Dee Foley, Jean Kallop, Charlotte Rounds, Dondrue Harrington, Evonne Lutkus, Debbie Feller (courtesy Bethlehem Central School District).

who wanted some. Also, juice and crackers were served each morning around 10:30. It would be many years before an actual kitchen facility would be built and allow students to buy hot lunches.

During the 1940s and 1950s, each teacher at Slingerlands School was assigned a specific area among the streets in the community. After the school day was over, the teachers visited each of the homes of school-aged children in their assigned areas to take the school census. It was also a great way to build a bond within the community. It is not known if each elementary school did this.

Personal bonds were certainly built in this community, as the Slingerlands School alumni appear to be the tightest knit of all the elementary schools. This was evidenced by the attendance at the school's 75th anniversary celebration in September 2017. Multiple generations

FIGURE 5-9 (LEFT) Slingerlands School 75th Anniversary celebration. Longtime school board member (now retired) Mrs. Lynne Lenhardt and former principal Mr. Dave Murphy (courtesy Slingerlands School).

FIGURE 5-10 (RIGHT) Slingerlands School 75th Anniversary celebration. The Hauser family. From l. to r.: Sally Hauser Miner '64, Doug Hauser '72, Scott Hauser '66, Wendy Hauser Liebl '76. Missing is Rebecca Hauser Hodgkinson '69, who passed away in 1981 (courtesy Wendy Hauser Liebl '76).

FIGURE 5-11 Slingerlands School 75th Anniversary celebration. Former student Mr. Doug Hauser '72 (courtesy Slingerlands School).

of former students descended upon the school to pay homage and to revisit the site of their youthful exploits (Figures 5-9, 5-10, and 5-11).

Several recalled the traditional fifth-grade musical, in which all fifth graders are included. These musicals were successfully enhanced by Mrs. Virginia Dale Spelich, who taught music for decades at Slingerlands school (Figure 5-12). Mrs. Spelich was known for ensuring the shows were top quality. The love for the musicals is personified by the rows of photos of each production lining the school's hallways. Perusing the photos is akin to walking back in time (Figures 5-13 and 5-14).

Another name mentioned often is that of Mr. William Morrison, who taught fifth and sixth grades at Slingerlands for many years before moving to the Middle School to teach sixth grade. Mr. Morrison was known to inspire his students to think, and for his compassion and empathy toward his students (Figure 5-15). One important student memory involved the fateful day of November 22, 1963. A student recalled that the principal knocked at the door and Mr. Morrison stepped out. When Mr. Morrison stepped back in, his eyes were

FIGURE 5-12 (LEFT) Mrs. Virginia Dale Spelich, longtime music teacher and creative force behind the Slingerlands fifth-grade musicals (courtesy Slingerlands School).

FIGURE 5-13 (RIGHT) Slingerlands School 75th Anniversary celebration. The Hauser family. From l. to r.: Sally Hauser Miner '64, Doug Hauser '72, Scott Hauser '66, Wendy Hauser Liebl '76. Missing is Rebecca Hauser Hodgkinson '69, who passed away in 1981 (courtesy Wendy Hauser Liebl).

clouded with tears. He assumed the responsibility of telling his students the President of the United States had been assassinated in Dallas that afternoon. All students were dismissed early that afternoon. Mr. Morrison immigrated to the United States from Scotland as a boy. During World War II he was a member of the revered 10th Mountain Division, the Ski Troops. In addition to his passion for teaching, he was instrumental in helping to create the Heldeberg Workshop, which has provided summer experiences for thousands of children since its inception in the early 1960s. Workshops were offered in a multitude of interesting areas (Science, Art, Performing Arts, Outdoor Education, etc.) (Figure 5-16). Mr. Morrison also worked tire-

FIGURE 5-14 (LEFT) More photos from past musicals (courtesy Andrew Baker).

FIGURE 5-15 (RIGHT) Slingerlands School 75th Anniversary celebration. Former teachers Mr. William Morrison and his daughter Mrs. Bonnie O'Shea (courtesy Bethlehem Central School District).

lessly, even after his retirement, with many school-based theater tech crews to enhance performances.

A discussion of the "early" years of Slingerlands school would not be complete without the mention of Mrs. Edna Ableman. Mrs. Ableman taught at Slingerlands for many years (1947–1975) and lived right near the school. Former students speak of her as though she had magical powers. Students under her tutelage who had been unable to read upon entering second grade passed to third grade as readers. One former student related that not only was he a new student in her class, but he was also absent due to various illnesses that year. Though out of class for weeks and months at a time, he said Mrs. Ableman made him feel part of the class despite his prolonged absences. She was sensitive to his needs. When it was suggested to hold the student back at the end

FIGURE 5-16 Heldeberg Workshop sign (courtesy Heldebergworkshop.org).

of the school year, Mrs. Ableman arranged to tutor the student at her home throughout the summer. The former student offered this wonderful tribute: "...Mrs. Ableman transferred something to me that is so much more vital than math or spelling. Her strength gave me strength. Without coddling, she made me feel safe, not just in class, but in life." This student also mentioned he was in awe of Mrs. Ableman's son Dick, who was tall and a basketball star. Dick graduated in the BCHS Class of 1962 and went on to star in basketball at Syracuse University along with his classmate, Rex Trobridge.

FIGURE 5-17 Slingerlands School and its current principal, Mr. Andrew Baker (courtesy Bethlehem Central School District).

Slingerlands Elementary was also fortunate to enjoy stability at the principal level. Since 1941, there have been just five principals: Mr. James Smith, Miss Mary Bida, Mrs. Virginia Lowe, Mr. David Murphy, and Mrs. Heidi Bonacquist. Other faculty and staff who enjoyed lengthy careers are Mrs. Katie DePorte, Mrs. Evonne Lutkus, Mr. Bernie Hungerford, and Mrs. Muriel Hungerford, to name just a few. Slingerlands Elementary lives up to its motto: A Very Special Place (Figure 5-17).

FIGURE 6-1 Map showing Babcock Corners on the upper right. 1856 Gould Map of Bethlehem (courtesy *Bethlehem Revisited*).

CHAPTER 6

GLENMONT SCHOOL

HISTORY SHOWS THAT SETTLEMENTS grow up around crossroads. Such is the case with Bethlehem Center, originally known as Babcock's Corners, located at the intersection of Route 9W and Feura Bush Road. It is now included as part of the hamlet of Glenmont. This is interesting because many residents might assume the area was always part of Glenmont. However, Floyd Brewer, author of *Bethlehem Revisited*, says "...Glenmont is located further east and near the Hudson at the intersection of Route 144 (River Road) and Glenmont Rd (313)" (Figure 6-1).

Raising money to build newer and larger schools was as much an issue in the past as it is today. The Common School system dictated that each district be financially independent. Any amount of funds collected was reliant on the residents within each district. Therefore, the number of inhabitants impacted the available amount to be collected and used for educational purposes.

The original one-room schoolhouse in Bethlehem Center (present-day Glenmont) was built prior to the Civil War. A growing population in 1880 caused a need for the existing tiny school to be replaced. Approximately $1,300 was raised to build a new school. The call for a still larger school became necessary in the early 1920s when the City of Albany annexed part of the Town of Bethlehem (Figure 6-2). The one-room schoolhouse serving the Kenwood area (School District No.12) was absorbed by the city. Therefore, any children living south of the Normanskill Creek had to transfer to the Bethlehem Center School, which was already overcrowded (Figure 6-3).

FIGURE 6-2 Original Bethlehem Center School in front of the newer school built in 1925 (courtesy Town of Bethlehem).

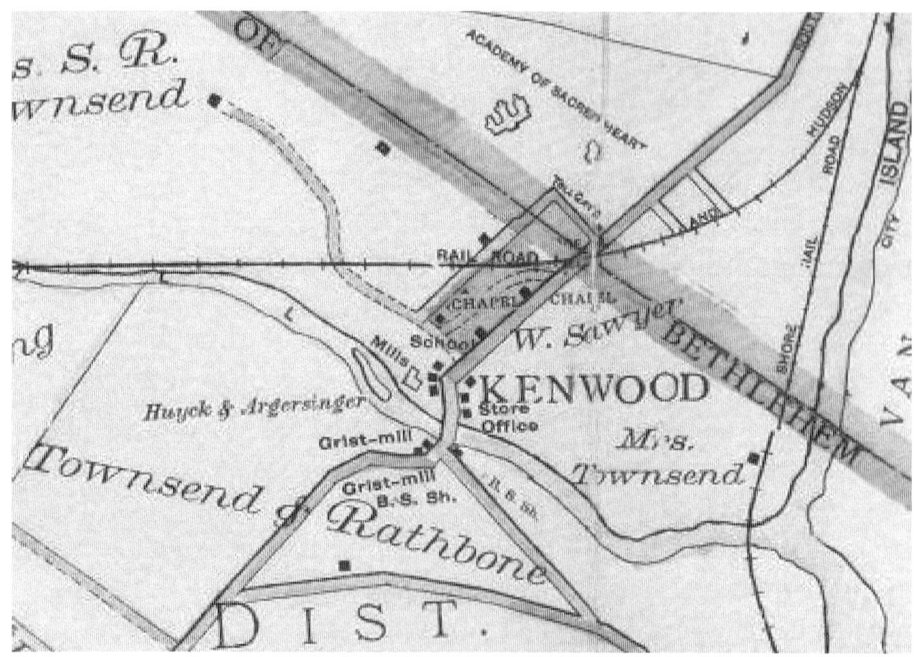

FIGURE 6-3 1891 map showing the Kenwood area as part of the Town of Bethlehem before the City of Albany absorbed the land north of the Normans Kill in 1910 (courtesy Wikipedia).

FIGURE 6-4 Bethlehem Center (Glenmont) School after it was purchased and operated privately as Bethlehem Pre-School (Courtesy David Bulnes '77).

At a cost of $40,000, a three-room school was built in 1925 directly behind the old one facing Route 9W. In time the old school building was torn down. The Bethlehem Center School housed all eight grades for many years and was one of the seven Common School Districts to merge and form Bethlehem Central Schools in 1930. The Bethlehem Center building was used by the district until the current Glenmont School opened its doors in May 1957. After that, the building was used as needed for kindergarten classes for several years (Figure 6-4). The Bethlehem Center School building is still in use today. It has housed the Bethlehem Preschool since 1976 and has been run for the last few decades by two BCSD alumnae.

During the building of Glenmont Elementary, in 1956–57, first- and second-grade students remained at the Bethlehem Center site (Figure 6-5). The school's two third grades were housed at Hamagrael, the two fourth grades inhabited Elsmere, the two fifth grades occupied space at Slingerlands, and the lone sixth grade took up residence at Delmar. The two kindergarten sessions took place daily at the Slingerlands Methodist Church. Overseeing all of this from her principal's office at the

FIGURE 6-5 Bethlehem Center School first grade (before 1957) (courtesy Facebook).

Bethlehem Center School was the district's first female principal, Mrs. Grace Erkson. While the newest Glenmont School was under construction, and many of her students were housed at other schools temporarily, Mrs. Erkson regularly traveled to each of the other schools to monitor her students (Figure 6-6).

In May of 1957, all 267 pupils, along with 12 teachers and support staff, were able to move into the new building. One activity at the present site of Glenmont School was to have the students plant a long row of pine seedlings in honor of the first Earth Day, April 22, 1970.

Glenmont School is unique due to its location on a heavily traveled road. Though set back quite a distance from Route 9W, the road continues to be busy with commercial and personal traffic (Figure 6-7). However, when it was built the area was largely devoid of commercial construction. Across the street from the school location was a large property that was used as a farm. In fact, when the Bethlehem Archeology Group

"FAMILY NIGHT MOVIE THEATRE" — Mrs. Wiltsey (4th gr. teach.) Mrs. Erkson, Principal, and Miss Marcia Pardoe (Third gr. Teacher) enjoy a collection of old telephones which were on exhibit at the Glenmont Elementary School.

FIGURE 6-6 Well-known teachers and principal posing for Glenmont School's "Family Night Movie Theatre." (l. to r.) Mrs. Wiltsey, Mrs. Erkson, and Miss Pardoe (courtesy Glenmont School Scrapbook).

was active, Glenmont students assisted them with digs on the property during the 1980s. Much of that property is now commercially developed though a parcel of land, designated as the Schiffendecker Farm Preserve and under the guidance of the Mohawk Hudson Land Conservancy, is maintained as a dedicated green space (Figure 6-8).

Part of the charm of the original location was its proximity to the large crossroad formed by the intersection of Route 9W and Feura Bush Road. Prior to the opening of the New York State Thruway, Route 9W was a major truck route and the main thoroughfare to New York City on this side of the Hudson River.

In the Bethlehem Center School's early years, students made the nearby blacksmith's shop a popular place to stop and visit. At one time in the early days, there was a house that served as the original tollgate

FIGURE 6-7 Aerial photo with Glenmont School pictured in the bottom half of the photo (courtesy Glenmont School Scrapbook).

for that portion of the plank road. The toll was ten cents per horse. As the years passed, a gas station took up residence at one of the corners. There has been a gas station at that corner ever since.

During the early 1960s the Bethlehem Center School was utilized as a home base for all kindergarten classes. Since kindergarten was run in half-day sessions, the small school was able to meet the district's needs. A highlight in students' memories from that time was the Circus presented in the spring by Mrs. Weiss' classes. The staging took place on the grounds behind the Bethlehem Center School. It was a popular event and was even covered by the local newspaper (Figures 6-9 and 6-10).

Other fond memories of school days at Glenmont School include (but are not limited to): field trips to Lawson's Lake as part of the Outdoor Education curriculum; saving waxed paper sandwich wrappers to "grease" the large playground slide; epic dodgeball games; chalkboard eraser fights; movie nights; and the end-of-year brown-bag picnic consisting of peanut butter and jelly sandwiches and small bags of Wise po-

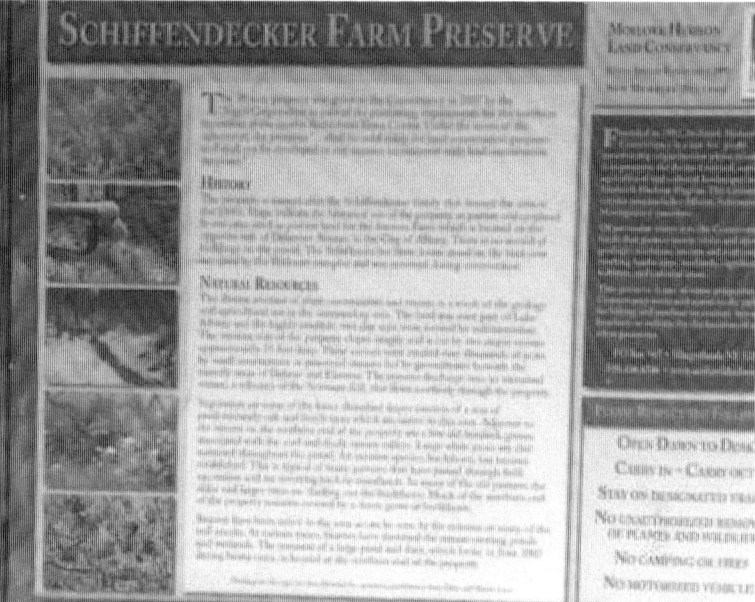

FIGURE 6-8 Sign denoting the Schiffendecker Farm Preserve near the Glenmont School property (courtesy Wikipedia).

FIGURE 6-9 Glenmont Circus participants: l. to r. Pamela Lewis, Susan Ford, Jenay Benanati, Lisa Momberger. All are the class of 1976 (courtesy Lisa Momberger '76).

FIGURE 6-10 More circus participants: Steve Healey '76, Dorothy Lindsay, Henry Heilmann, Karl Pittz '77, and Cary Dibble (courtesy Lisa Momberger '76).

tato chips (Figure 6-11). Many teachers are remembered fondly by former students. Some names mentioned frequently are Mr. Brown, Miss Pardoe, Mrs. Fuller, Mr. Austin, Miss Samuelson, and Mrs. Edmonds.

Another staff member recalled by many former students was a custodian known as Smitty. Smitty worked at the school in the 1960s and 1970s and was known to flood an area of pavement outdoors during the winter so students could ice skate during lunch recess. It is also reported that Smitty often turned the outdoor lights on in the evenings so kids could ice skate after school hours.

Looking through a well-maintained school scrapbook reveals several items of importance. A 1963 article from The Spotlight sports the headline, "Nancy Tudico Awarded First Annual Glenmont School Scholarship." Miss Tudico would receive a $300 grant in two installments (Figure 6-12). An alternate, George Parry, was also named. Both

FIGURE 6-11 Third grade class picture, circa 1967. Mrs. Howe is the teacher (courtesy Brian Woolford '76).

had been Glenmont School students. A mimeographed cover of a PTA Handbook from 1955–56 displays The Bethlehem Center School's "theme" from that time: Child-School-Community. Their Future (Figure 6-13).

As with other elementary schools in the district, Glenmont employed at least two principals who remained at the school for lengthy periods of time. Mrs. Grace Erkson was principal from 1957–1972 and Mr. Donald Robillard was at the helm from 1973–1995. Both came from within the ranks of the district's schools.

Mrs. Erkson taught at both Elsmere School and, in its first year of existence, Hamagrael School. Her transition to principal at the Glenmont School provided the school with a veteran leader to ensure the success of the school's new location. It also gave the district its first female principal. At the time, students were accustomed to seeing female teachers but not a female principal. A quote from Mrs. Erkson's 2009 obituary tells us she "was a powerful role model for women and made significant contributions to the lives of students during her career." Mrs. Erkson saw the school through a fifteen-year span of time, serving as principal from 1957–1972.

NANCY TUDICO AWARDED FIRST ANNUAL GLENMONT SCHOOL SCHOLARSHIP

Nancy J. Tudico, daughter of Mr. and Mrs. Paul Tudico of Glenmont, a former sixth grade pupil at the Glenmont Elementary School and a senior at Bethlehem Central School in Delmar, has been awarded the first Glenmont PTA Scholarship Grant. The award represents $300 which will be given to Miss Tudico in two payments; one in September, the other prior to the beginning of the second semester of the student's freshmen year in college.

Miss Tudico has been active in the Future Teachers of America Club as Chaplain and a member of its Activities Committee, chairman of the Points Committee and president of the Club in her senior year.

She is on the School Year Book Staff, has been a member of the Spanish Club and in her junior year was a participant in the Canteen Show.

Music activities include membership in the concert choir for 3 years, the Chansonettes, the Choraliers and the Starlighters.

The alternate chosen by the Scholarship Selection Committee of the Bethlehem Senior High School is George Kondred Parry, son of Mr. and Mrs. George Parry of Feura Bush Road, Delmar, also a former Glenmont Elementary School pupil.

The Glenmont PTA will continue to present this award annually to a Bethlehem Senior who has completed the final two years of his elementary school at Glenmont. The selection is based on sincerity of desire of the student to continue his education and scholastic achievement.

Soon after the Glenmont School was established in 1956, its PTA concluded that a scholarship program for students was the one worthy project it wished to promote. A Scholarship Committee was formed and worked for several years formulating procedures to be followed in establishing the Scholarship as an annual award.

Nancy J. Tudico

PTA members and many friends of the school in the vicinity of Glenmont have given countless hours to the PTA's major money raising event, the Glenmont Variety Show which was presented annually under the direction of John Schoch for the past four years. Receipts from bake sales and contributions received from a dance group, the Helderberg Twirlers, have helped the PTA reach its financial goal and made the scholarship program possible.

The formal presentation of the award to Miss Tudico will be made on March 14 at 8:00 p.m. at the Glenmont School. Taking part in the presentation will be Mr. Carl Kundel, PTA president, Mr. Richard Hussey, chairman of the Scholarship Committee, and Miss Ruth Doyle, sixth grade teacher at the time Miss Tudico was at Glenmont.

FIGURE 6-12 First Glenmont School scholarship winner, Nancy Tudico '63 (courtesy Glenmont School Scrapbook).

FIGURE 6-13 (LEFT) Cover of PTA program 1955–1956 (courtesy Glenmont School Scrapbook).

FIGURE 6-14 (RIGHT) Mr. Donald Robillard, longtime Glenmont School principal (courtesy Glenmont School).

Her successor, Mr. Donald Robillard, would see the school through its next twenty-two years, serving as principal from 1973–1995 (Figure 6-14). Mr. Robillard was another veteran teacher, having spent time teaching at Elsmere School and as principal at Watervliet High School. His principalship was very meaningful to him. A passage from his 2020 obituary states, "Under his Glenmont leadership, he guided the school to the district's first National Blue-Ribbon School of Excellence recognition. He promoted a motto of 'Care about yourself: Care about the people and things around you.' His legacy of outstanding accomplishments will have a lasting effect on Glenmont Elementary School, its many teachers, staff, parents and students."

One of the original fifteen common schools in the district, located near the intersection of Feura Bush Road and Route 9W for over one hundred years, the Bethlehem Center School made the transition to a new location down the road and to a new name. Glenmont Elementary School continues to thrive after more than sixty years in its current location.

HAMAGRAEL PARK IN DELMAR

Open House Sunday, 2 to 5

See this fine quality 67' brick and frame rambler on a large wooded corner plot offered at a sensible price of $21,800. It includes a center hall layout, 21' living room with dining ell, custom built kitchen with G.E. cabinets and breakfast corner, 3 bedrooms with high level windows and floor-to-ceiling storage wall closets and a two-compartment tile bath. Powder dry basement completely tile drained and waterproofed, full attic with walk-up stairs, 2-car attached garage. Lawns, drive, storms and screens included. $6,000 cash; $92.43 per month. Decorated to a king's taste and available for immediate possession.

DIRECTIONS: Turn left off Delaware Ave. on Winne Road and look for "Open House" signs at end of street.

HOME CONSTRUCTION CORP.
"Community Developers"

4-1172   PHILIP E. ROBERTS   4-1172
Exclusive Sales Agent

FIGURE 7-1 Advertisement for Hamagrael Park real estate (courtesy *Albany Times Union*).

CHAPTER 7

HAMAGRAEL SCHOOL

DESPITE THE NATIONWIDE DEPRESSION in the 1930s, Delmar was growing in leaps and bounds. New housing was under construction throughout the town of Bethlehem. One development that appears repeatedly in the newspapers from that time is Hamagrael Park (Figure 7-1).

The development was touted as being a community within a community. It was to contain its own park and skating pond for use by residents of the 266-unit neighborhood. As people moved to the area, it quickly became apparent a new elementary school would be needed. Delmar and Elsmere Schools were bursting at the seams by the mid-to-late 1940s, as was the junior/senior high.

An 18-acre parcel of property adjacent to Hamagrael Park was purchased by the BCSD in 1942. Not only was supervising principal Hamilton Bookhout a forward thinker, so was the Board of Education. Advertising and construction began in the new development in the late 1930s. It seems even though the Great Depression overshadowed virtually every community during the 1930s, it did not hinder development within the Town of Bethlehem, especially in Delmar.

As to the derivation of the unusual name of Hamagrael, there has been wide speculation over the years. The story of Hamagrael's name, long a subject of curiosity, appears at the end of this chapter thanks to former BCHS graduate John Yacobian (class of 1981), who conducted a tremendous amount of research to solve this mystery.

FIGURE 7-2 The newly built Hamagrael School, circa 1954. Note the dirt roads (courtesy Town of Bethlehem).

Though Hamagrael has its roots firmly planted in the distant past, the development and the school were conceived with the future in mind. New homes in the Hamagrael area were heavily advertised throughout the 1950s and 60s. One article in the *Times Union* from 1953 touted homes in the Winne Road area (nearer the school) as being priced between $18,500 and $21,500. The article also reports many lots on Wisconsin Avenue and Albin Road were graded and ready for building. Since median income in 1953 was $4,000, the homes were affordable for many. Also mentioned in the article was the upcoming construction of the new $750,000 elementary school.

By 1953, total district enrollment had doubled in the twenty years since centralization. Student population was approaching 2,500, with over 1,500 in the elementary schools alone. Back in the late 1920s when the new Delmar and Elsmere Schools were built, it was widely thought they would "never be filled"; fast forward almost 25 years and all elementary schools were at or above capacity. With a new high school facility (complete with swimming pool) under construction, supervising principal Hamilton Bookhout gained approval for a new elementary school (Hamagrael), as well as for a $458,000 expansion at Slingerlands.

FIGURE 7-3 The cover of the *McGuffey Reader*, a schoolbook used nationwide. It was the inspiration for the name McGuffey Lane (courtesy Wikipedia).

Hamagrael opened in September of 1954 and welcomed 380 students (Figure 7-2). The fourteen new classrooms were lacking some hardware, fixtures, and trim, but the students embraced their new school. The principal was Mr. John Falvey who had spent the previous three years as principal at Clarksville. Hamagrael was the epitome of a neighborhood school, completely ensconced in a residential area; it did not have the challenges of a busy road like Delaware Avenue or Route 9W out front. The school is located on McGuffey Lane, named after William Holmes McGuffey, the author of the *McGuffey Readers*, a series of books that were widely used in elementary schools as students learned to read (Figure 7-3). Delmar resident John Glenn, a longtime member of the Board of Education, had traveled to Ohio to obtain the books for the Hamagrael students.

Hamagrael was quick to embrace the concept of mainstreaming. Mainstreaming occurs when special needs students, who had previously been taught in isolation, are included in the regular classroom with some additional support. An article in *The Knickerbocker News*, dated May 21, 1958, featured the story of Tommy Smith, a blind student in the second grade. His parents decided to send him to public school rather than sending him away to a residential school for the blind as was usually done at that time. Tommy's father explained in the article, "Instead of sending him away to a residential school—where the problems of adjustment at school followed by readjustment when he comes home would make themselves felt-we decided it is better to adapt to his own neighbor children."

Mainstreaming special needs students was not common in the late 1950s, but Hamagrael School would continue a practice of educating children with vision problems. Another blind student was highlighted again in *The Knickerbocker News* in June 1967. Ironically, his name was also Tom; he was also referred to as Tommy. Tom Winship had attended residential schools for the blind until he entered Hamagrael as a third grader. He missed his family while away at school and thus became a student at Hamagrael (Figure 7-4). The premise of the article discussed his innate ability in sculpting animals he had never seen. As Tom grew older, he successfully navigated the maze of corridors within the Middle School and the High School. He was an excellent musician and very proficient with the guitar.

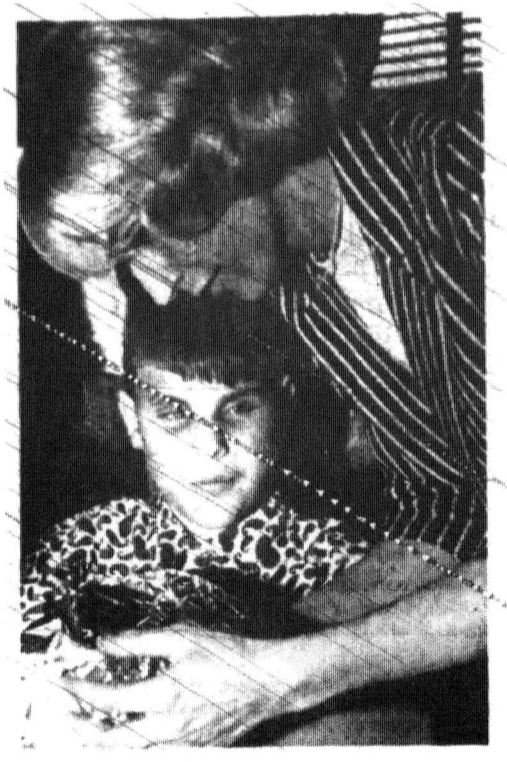

"SEEING" COMES DIFFERENTLY — A fourth grader at Hamagrael School in Delmar, Tommy Winship is particularly adept in forming objects in clay and other media although he has never seen them. Sightless since birth, Tommy depends on description and feel to create realistic conceptions of the world around him. His teacher, Mrs. Muriel Heicklen, finds he fits easily into her class room routine.

FIGURE 7-4 Hamagrael School was known for its instructional program for visually impaired students. Pictured here is Tommy Winship, circa 1966 (not to be confused with another student named Tommy Smith who was a blind student in the late 1950s at Hamagrael) (courtesy *Albany Times Union*).

Each mainstreamed student was as much a part of the regular classroom as any student, though some did receive specialized instruction in a few disciplines such as math and reading. A couple of Tommy Smith's elementary teachers took supplemental summer courses with expenses paid through the

National Foundation for the Blind and the Delmar Lions Club. Proceeds from a theater production put on by the Slingerlands Players were donated to the Lion's Club to assist with this endeavor.

Hamagrael's location is unique in that it is embedded in a large residential neighborhood. While a few other schools—Delmar, Elsmere, and Slingerlands—are situated in neighborhoods, the Hamagrael neighborhood literally grew up with its school. Woods border the property on one side and along the rear of the school's outdoor area (Figures 7-5 and 7-6).

FIGURE 7-5 (LEFT) Front entrance of Hamagrael School (courtesy Bethlehem Central School District).

FIGURE 7-6 (RIGHT) Front of the school featuring the historical marker noting the burial of an American revolution soldier, Lt. John Leonard (courtesy Beth Anderson).

Behind the school runs a dirt road, known to locals as the "water line," which runs from Feura Bush to the Delaware Plaza and beyond. Pipes carry water to Albany from the filtration plant in Feura Bush. The water originates from the Alcove Reservoir and supplies the city of Albany.

Many a youth in this town has his or her own stories about the "water line." It was a great way to access Delaware Plaza without having to ride bikes along Delaware Avenue. Many youthful rites of passage may or may not have occurred along the long dirt road. Suffice it to say that children used it for bicycling and riding minibikes and ATVs, as well as various and sundry social gatherings. Almost every school in the district possesses one of these spots and they have probably all been used in the same manner since the building of the schools.

Similar to other schools in the district, Hamagrael enjoyed continuity with its principals. The first principal, Mr. John Falvey, came to the district in 1946 and served as the principal of the Bethlehem Center (Glenmont) School from 1946–49. He then served as principal of Clarksville School for four years before assuming the principalship of Hamagrael School when it opened in 1954. Mr. Falvey remained at the helm until his retirement in 1976 (Figure 7-7). Mr. Falvey was an active member of the community and served as the Director of Continuing Education for many years. He was respected and well-liked by students, parents, and teachers.

Ironically, his retirement in 1976 resolved an issue the district was facing with the closure of Delmar Elementary. It allowed Mr. Joseph Schaefer, principal at Delmar School during its last year of operation, to become principal at Hamagrael. Mr. Schaefer had been principal at Clarksville School, having come from the Guilderland District where he had served first as a teacher and then as principal at Guilderland Elementary.

Prior to Mr. Falvey's retirement, Mr. Schaefer was to return to Clarks-

JOHN J. FALVEY, PRINCIPAL, HAMAGRAEL AND BETHLEHEM CENTER ELEMENTARY SCHOOLS

John J. Falvey, Principal of the Hamagrael Elementary School, is one of the better known principals in our district. During the past ten years he has been associated with four of our elementary schools; first as teacher in Delmar, later as principal of the Clarksville Elementary School, and more recently as principal of both Hamagrael and Bethlehem Center Elementary Schools. Educated in Kingston, New York, he received his baccalaureate and master degrees in elementary education at New Paltz State Teachers College. Following graduation he taught four years in schools in New York State outside of the Bethlehem Central District, served an additional four years with Uncle Sam, and since 1946 he has served as teacher and principal in our district.

FIGURE 7-7 Longtime Hamagrael principal, Mr. John Falvey (courtesy Glenmont School scrapbook).

ville School where Mr. David Murphy was serving as the interim principal. Had this happened, since Mr. Murphy had the least seniority, he would have had to serve as an assistant principal. Clarksville residents had signed a petition to retain Mr. Murphy as principal and were very pleased when Mr. Murphy was allowed to retain his job as principal.

Mr. Schaefer, in an interview, acknowledged that the decision to close Delmar School "broke everyone's hearts." Enrollment was declining and the building was in disrepair. Mr. Schaefer faced a challenge as he left an established school with a veteran teaching staff for a newer school with a younger faculty. The position at Hamagrael challenged Mr. Schaefer to be a "hands-on" administrator who was able to hire much of the faculty during his eighteen years as principal.

FIGURE 7-8 Playground behind Hamagrael School (courtesy Bethlehem Central School District).

Since the Hamagrael neighborhood grew over time along with the school, there were many young professionals sending their children to the school, and those parents had high expectations for their children's achievement. Due to the tone that Hamilton Bookhout set from the beginning, not only are expectations high for student success but they are also high for the quality of the faculty and staff.

One distinct feature of the one-story Hamagrael School is that many classrooms feature a door that opens directly to the outdoors. This design was for safety and allowed those within the classroom easy egress in the event of a fire. Many former students shared stories of family dogs walking to school with them. When the weather was nice, teachers opened the doors for ventilation. More than one teacher over the years allowed a beloved pet to hang out in the classroom (Figure 7-8).

FIGURE 7-9 Miss Sammie (the spelling of "Sammy" used by Findagrave.com is incorrect) Ives, a very innovative and much-loved teacher (courtesy Findagrave.com).

As with all the other schools in the district, Hamagrael's footprint has increased over the years. Since it opened there have been additions and renovations, but many former students would still recognize their school immediately from its distinctive façade. In fact, veteran principal Mr. Dave Ksanznak (retired June 2021) reports many former students stop and visit their former school. The students may have referred to their elementary school jokingly as "Hamajail Elementary Penitentiary," but most students enjoyed their time there.

Several students who attended Hamagrael during the late 1950s into the 1960s were quick to recall a particular teacher named Miss Sammie Ives (Figure 7-9). Miss Ives spent thirteen years at Hamagrael, from 1956 to 1968, and primarily taught fifth grade. Students remembered she was a proponent of the use of creativity across the curriculum. While it may be prevalent now, it was rather novel for the late 1950s. For example, Miss Ives would pair a lesson in art with one in music. Former students said it made their learning "real" and inspired them to learn more. Various newspaper articles from the time revealed a great deal about her singing prowess (always a plus at the elementary level), her participation in civic organizations, and her planning and teaching in innumerable workshops for educators. After leaving Hamagrael, Miss Ives took more of an administrative position with the two Colonie school districts, in which she oversaw special education classes. She was also a student teaching supervisor for Plattsburgh State (now SUNY Plattsburgh) at the time of her unexpected death in 1973. Miss Ives is but one example of fine teachers in both districts.

Hamagrael remains a very active elementary school. There are many theories as to how the school got its name, but the following pages will shed light on this mystery.

FIGURE JY7-1

FIGURE JY7-2

HAMAGRAEL ELEMENTARY
A Family, a Farm, and How a School Was Named

BY JOHN YACOBIAN

INTRODUCTION

As students attending Hamagrael Elementary school in Delmar, New York, we used to refer to our school as "Hamajail." Although it seemed humorous to us at the time, we never really considered the origins of the name of our school. The thought never crossed our minds about how unique we were, as the only students on the planet going to a school named Hamagrael. What we did notice is how difficult it was to spell the name of the school, which resembled no other word. So how did Hamagrael actually get its name, and what does it mean? I recall being told it had something to do with native peoples. Although indigenous populations were known to be in the area around Hamagrael, the origins of the name are actually connected to homes in Delmar, New York and Worcester, Massachusetts, and the families who lived in them.

THE GODDARD FAMILY

To understand the history of Hamagrael's name, we must travel over a century back in time and 130 miles east to Worcester, Massachusetts. At the dawn of the twentieth century Worcester was a bustling industrial city, teeming with immigrants toiling in factories turning out wire and nails. Harry Goddard (Figure JY7-3) was one of Worcester's industrial pioneers. Born in 1863, Goddard worked himself up, laboring in many aspects of wire manufacturing. When Harry Goddard died in 1927, he owned and managed the thriving Spencer Wire Company,

FIGURE JY7-3
Harry Goddard (Courtesy
American Antiquarian Society)

FIGURE JY7-4
Marion Goddard (Courtesy
American Antiquarian Society)

FIGURE JY7-5
Grace Goddard (Courtesy
American Antiquarian Society)

FIGURE JY7-6
Eleanor Goddard (Courtesy
American Antiquarian Society)

which had nearly 1,000 employees. And it is from the first two letters of Harry Goddard's name that the first two letters of Hamagrael come.

Harry had two daughters, and Marian was the youngest. She was born in Worcester County, Massachusetts in 1893. Marian had always been in poor health. To escape the harsh New England winters, she would routinely travel south. In May 1918, Marian was headed home when the ship she was traveling on, the *City of Athens*, was struck by a French warship in the foggy waters off New Jersey. Marian, along with 65 other people on board, died in the watery disaster. She was only 24 years old. And so it is from Marion that the next two letters of Hamagrael originate.

G and R, the next two letters of the puzzle, come from the matriarch of the family, whose name was Grace. Grace Watson was born in 1866 in Spencer, Massachusetts. She is remembered for her generosity, and also for her role as president of the Spencer Wire company after her husband Harry's death in 1927. She ran Spencer Wire—a very unusual role for a woman during that time—until it was sold in 1933. Grace died in 1935.

Finally, the last two letters of the acronym, E and L, were contributed by Eleanor, Harry and Grace's first-born child. Born in 1899, she graduated from Smith College in 1911 and married F. Harold Daniels. Together they were very active in the social and cultural life of Worcester. Eleanor died in 1981.

This may leave some wondering if the Goddard family is related to Dr. Robert Goddard, who is credited with inventing the first liquid-fueled rocket. Dr. Goddard, who also lived in Worcester, was from the same family; he was a cousin to the Harry Goddard family.

THE HEINSOHN FAMILY

However, it is another Goddard cousin upon whom the story turns, and her name was Elizabeth Hall. Elizabeth Hall's mother was Harry Goddard's older sister, making Harry an uncle to Elizabeth. Elizabeth Hall and her cousins Marion and Eleanor Goddard grew up together in Worcester, sharing many experiences and fond memories through their childhood.

Elizabeth Hall was a remarkable woman. Born in Worcester, Massachusetts in 1896, she graduated from Oberlin College in 1919 and then started medical school at Yale. In 1920 Elizabeth decided to take a break from her studies and sail to China to visit her sister Marge, who was working there as a missionary and preparing for marriage. But as it would turn out, both sisters would have weddings in China after Elizabeth met and married Edwin Heinsohn, who was also working in Shanghai. Edwin, who was three years older than Elizabeth, was from Mount Vernon, New York. After the birth of the couple's first child, Judith, in China in 1922, the Heinsohns decided to move back to the United States because they felt it was a better place to raise their young family. They first settled in Topeka, Kansas, and Edwin soon found employment with the Seymour Packing Company.

FIGURE JY7-7
Elizabeth Hall Heinsohn (Photo courtesy of the Heinsohn Family)

FIGURE JY7-8
Edwin Heinsohn (Photo courtesy of the Heinsohn Family)

HAMAGRAEL FARM

The Delmar chapter of the story begins when Seymour Packing, Edwin's employer, sent him to Albany to open a sales office. In 1923 the

Heinsohns built a home on Adams Street in Delmar. Three more children— Barbara, Meredith, and Raymond, in 1924, 1927, and 1932 respectively—would add to the growing family. In early 1932 they decided to move to an old farm on the edge of Delmar, on present-day Roweland Avenue. It was a hundred-year-old structure set on 100 acres. The farmhouse needed work, and it took many months to remodel the two-story house into a home. Eventually they would name the property "Hamagrael Farm."

FIGURE JY7-9
Hamagrael Farm (Photo courtesy of the Heinsohn Family)

FIGURE JY7-10
Hamagrael Farmhouse
(Photo courtesy of the
Heinsohn Family)

FIGURE JY7-11
Hamagrael Farmhouse
(Photo courtesy of the
Heinsohn Family)

Thirty years after Eleanor's death, the Heinsohn family recalled that she said Hamagrael had been the name of the Goddard's summer home on a lake near Worcester, the name being based on the names of the Goddard family—Harry, Marion, Grace, and Eleanor. The passage of time, and the deaths of the Goddard and Heinsohn family members who would have had direct knowledge of this part of the story, make it difficult to corroborate. The house that Harry and Grace owned in Worcester—a house which is now part of the Worcester Antiquarian Society—was named "Elmarion," so there is a clear precedent for naming homes after family members. And we can say with certainty that the name Hamagrael does come from the Goddard family.

We do know that life for the Heinsohns in and around Hamagrael Farm was delightful. They entertained church groups for picnics and had corn roasts, hayrides for school classes, Halloween parties in their barns, skating on the back pond for youth groups and Campfire girls, and toboggan slides down the hill in the front.

HAMAGRAEL PARK

In 1937 Edwin Heinsohn decided to subdivide a portion of the land around his home. What motivated him is unknown, although this was the height of The Great Depression, and that may well have been a factor in his reasoning. Edwin did set down de-

FIGURE JY7-12
Barbara, Raymond, Elizabeth, Meredith, and Judith Heinsohn (Photo courtesy of the Heinsohn Family)

FIGURE JY7-13
Raymond, Meredith, Elizabeth, and Barbara Heinsohn, and Cannon
(Photo courtesy of the Heinsohn Family)

FIGURE JY7-14
Edwin, Barbara, Raymond, Judith, Meredith, and
Elizabeth Heinsohn in the Hamagrael living room, 1934
(Photo courtesy of the Heinsohn Family)

tailed restrictions about the style of homes that could be built, and even prohibited Poplar trees and overhead utilities lines from the lots. The area was called "Hamagrael Park." It included what would become the end of Roweland Avenue and Winne Road and parts of Jordan Boulevard. The lots were slow to develop and did not really take off until after World War II ended in 1945 and the returning soldiers needed homes in which to raise their baby boomer families. In 1942 the Heinsohns moved back to Topeka, Kansas; at about the same time, the Bethlehem Central School District acquired 18 acres of land at the end of Winne Road. The school that was subsequently built borrowed the name that Heinsohn had used in his development. The school building itself was not finished until 1954. Heinsohn continued to be involved in the development of land around the area as late as 1953. Edwin died in 1965 in Shawnee, Kansas, with his wife Elizabeth dying in 1986. The names "Hamagrael Park" and "Hamagrael Farm" have passed into history, but the legacy of the Harry Goddard and the Edwin Heinsohn families lives on through the tens of thousands of school children who have passed through the doors of Hamagrael Elementary School.

ACKNOWLEDGMENTS

This project would not have been possible without the assistance of the Heinsohn family. I want to especially thank Tina Pough, Raymond Hall Heinsohn's daughter, for her time, patience, and consideration with all my questions. She also graciously allowed me to use the Heinsohn family photo for this narrative. I also want to thank Judy Heinsohn Quinn and her daughter Betsy Quinn for their help.

The Goddard Family Home in Worcester, Massachusetts now houses the American Antiquarian Society (AAS), which includes many artifacts from the Goddard Family. I want to thank Ellen Dunlap, the president of the AAS, for her assistance with this project, and also for allowing me to use the Goddard Family portraits.

ABOUT THE AUTHOR

John Yacobian attended Hamagrael Elementary and has many fond recollections of the school, the fine teachers and staff, and the many friendships made there. It may have only been five years, just a small part of a lifetime, but those years still hold strong associations, memories, and impressions that resonate these many years later. John lives in New York City and is a producer with CBS News.

PHOTO CREDITS

The four photos of the Goddard family were used with the permission of the American Antiquarian Society expressly for this narrative, and cannot be used, borrowed or replicated without the permission of the owner.

The photos of the Heinsohn family and Hamagrael farm were used with the permission of the Heinsohn family expressly for this narrative, and cannot be used, borrowed or replicated without the permission of the owner.

FIGURE 8-1 Mr. W. Jack Weaver (courtesy *The Spotlight*).

CHAPTER 8

332 KENWOOD AVENUE

ONCE THE NEW BRIDGE, or viaduct as it was called, spanned the Normanskill in 1928, providing safe passage from Albany to Delmar and Elsmere, the population of the Town of Bethlehem began to increase at a steady rate. Though the district had opened Delmar High in 1926, schools throughout the town quickly became overcrowded.

A Delmar resident named Mr. W. Jack Weaver offered a viable solution. Mr. Weaver was born in 1890 near Mt. Washington, Massachusetts. His father was a farmer, a not uncommon occupation at the time. Mr. Weaver was able to attend Cornell University and earn a degree in agriculture education. Eventually he also received a master's degree. This was quite an accomplishment for a small-town boy. He married in 1914 and would have three children, all of whom would graduate from BCSD. By 1920 Jack was working for the New York State Education Department as an agricultural education supervisor (Figure 8-1).

Much of what Mr. Weaver did for State Ed was to travel throughout the state to evaluate the agricultural education programs. He began to see different districts emerge through the process of centralization and brought this idea to Delmar. As a result of discussions and presentations, he was able to convince the townspeople that centralization was needed. During the new district's first year of existence in 1930, it was apparent a new school was needed. (As an aside, the school budget for the first year after centralization was $44,040.)

FIGURE 8-2 Original plan for "new" high school, early 1930s (courtesy *Albany County Post*).

The four-year-old Delmar High building on the corner of Delaware and Borthwick Avenues was overflowing with students in grades 7–12. During the spring of 1930, the school board purchased property—once the Grebe chicken farm—on Kenwood Avenue for just under $30,000. Before the centralization, informal discussions revealed a new high school building could cost $325,000. It was on this premise the centralization was approved.

In early January of 1931, the Board of Education presented sketches, by a New York City architectural firm, of a wonderful school building complete with a price tag of $482,000. Town voters rejected this plan by a vote of 325–86. Residents were dismayed that an "outside" firm had been used instead of local architects. Mr. Jack Weaver, then president of the Board of Education, said in an *Altamont Enterprise* article "It is evident the taxpayers are entirely out of sympathy with plans of the board to employ NY architects and with a school building which is more costly than was anticipated a year ago. However, it is not to be considered that the residents are opposed to a new school building or better facilities" (Figure 8-2).

Indeed, the residents were not opposed; eventually, a bond of $317,000 was approved in 1932. Part of the school was occupied in the fall of 1933, and it was opened to all students in early 1934. Along with a larger school came the opportunity to expand the course offerings. Four

FIGURE 8-3 The new junior/senior high school, circa 1936 (courtesy *Oriole* yearbook).

MR. DONALD Z. TERHUNE

Universities: Syracuse, B.S.; Cornell; Michigan State, M.S.; Columbia; NYSCT, M.S.

Subjects: General Agriculture; Vocational Agriculture.

Adviser: School Garden Programs; F.F.A.

FIGURE 8-4 Mr. Donald Terhune, agriculture teacher (courtesy *Oriole* yearbook).

core courses—English, Civics/History, Math, and Science—had always been taught; now additional courses such as French, Latin, art, music, and physical education could be offered. In the latter part of the 1930s, agriculture and commerce (business) were added. Mr. Donald Terhune was the full-time agriculture teacher from 1936 until the curriculum was dropped in 1959. BCHS maintained an active chapter of Future Farmers of America (FFA) during that time (Figures 8-3 and 8-4).

It must be said that, during the early years of centralization and growth, the Bethlehem Central School District was fortunate to employ a series of outstanding administrators. The first was Mr. Olin Bouck. He began as a teacher in District No. 10 in 1925 and taught in the Delmar School when it was located on Kenwood Avenue (the present-day Masonic Temple). By the following year he was appointed principal of the brand-new Delmar High, located on the corner of Delaware and Borthwick Avenues. Mr. Bouck was eventually plucked from the district in 1931 to become a district superintendent. His job was to oversee four local school districts: Bethlehem, Guilderland, and two districts in Colonie. Mr. Bouck worked as an educator for 45 years (Figure 8-5).

FIGURE 8-5 Mr. Olin Bouck, who served as a teacher, principal, and superintendent of four school districts (courtesy *Oriole* yearbook).

The district still benefited from Mr. Bouck's overarching influence as superintendent, and another very effective educator stepped into Mr. Bouck's shoes within the district. Mr. Heth Coons was with the district for eight years during the 1930s. He guided the faculty and the students through the new school's construction as well as the expansion of the school's curriculum. His success in Bethlehem led to his departure in 1938 to take a job as Superintendent of Schools in Amsterdam, New York, a job he held for just five years before his unexpected death at the age of 53 (Figure 8-6).

FIGURE 8-6 Mr. Heth Coons was a teacher and principal for several years before leaving for an administrative post in Amsterdam, New York (courtesy *Oriole* yearbook).

FIGURE 8-7 Mr. Hamilton Bookhout, longtime principal, and superintendent (courtesy *Oriole* yearbook).

Mr. Coons' departure led to another individual stepping in to fill the leadership void in 1938; this person would have a profound effect on the Bethlehem Central School District for decades. His name was Mr. Hamilton Bookhout, and he helmed the district from 1938 until his retirement in 1964. An article from the *Altamont Enterprise* on September 2, 1938, announced "Bookhout, New Head of BCHS, Assumes Job." He was described as a supervising principal and his responsibilities were to oversee the entire school district of 65 teachers and 1500 students in addition to serving as principal of the high school (Figure 8-7). The article claimed Mr. Bookhout was well-suited for the job. He was a graduate of Hamilton College and Columbia University. Mr. Bookhout initially taught on Long Island before moving to the school district in Holland Patent, New York, where he oversaw their centralization process.

As the *Altamont Enterprise* article stated further, "The guiding work Bookhout will do at Delmar is aimed principally at working out an educational program for each pupil which will give him the most, and then adjust his school program to that. He explains that this system takes into consideration the capabilities of boys and girls. He points out that it is better

FIGURE 8-8 Early view of the Kenwood Avenue campus (courtesy *Oriole* yearbook).

for them to graduate with diplomas in special subjects rather than for them to fail to get a college entrance diploma." Though Mr. Bookhout had some detractors over the years, an overwhelming majority of his teachers and students held him in high esteem.

Mr. Hamilton Bookhout was viewed as a visionary. He pushed the board to buy land periodically, thus enabling expansion of the district whenever the need arose. He also had a "forest" planted that was designed to provide trees for all the district schools. There is no way to verify this last bit of information, though several different people spoke of it. Also, it is unknown where this area was located. It has been suggested it may have been the area behind the junior/senior high school between the former football field and the play fields. Again, there has been no way to verify this information, and a photo from 1936 does not support that theory (Figure 8-8).

Mr. Bookhout was very invested in his students and in his teachers. A student from the class of 1944 spoke of playing hooky once during her high school years. She was called in to Mr. Bookhout's office, where he expressed his disappointment in her. All these decades later she explained that what he said was worse than any punishment he could have meted out.

FIGURE 8-9 Mr. Hamilton Bookhout, principal, and Mr. William Kinsley, assistant principal (courtesy *Oriole* yearbook).

It was well known that Mr. Bookhout put his students and teachers first. He had an open-door policy and was allowed to be interrupted even during meetings. Mr. Bookhout was known to recruit his teachers directly from the student teaching supervisors at Albany State. The supervisors at Albany State knew Mr. Bookhout expected the best, so they often sent him the "cream of the crop."

During Mr. Bookhout's tenure, the Bethlehem Central School District built three new elementary schools, a new high school, and added many additions to each school. Lest we think Mr. Bookhout was no mere mortal, a brief article in the *Altamont Enterprise* dated May 29, 1953, reported that the supervising principal was ill and being temporarily replaced by Mr. William C. Kinsley (Figure 8-9). The president of the Board of Education stated, "Hamilton H. Bookhout, supervising principal of the BCSD, has had a mild heart attack, brought on by over-exertion." Thankfully Mr. Bookhout resumed his duties and continued in the supervising principal position until his retirement in 1964.

FIGURE 8-10 An early view of the front of the school. The beautiful arched windows remain a prevalent feature (courtesy *Oriole* yearbook).

And now, back to the historical context surrounding the construction of this school. The original footprint of the school would seem tiny compared to its present size, but in 1934 the new school must have seemed fabulous (Figures 8-10, 8-11, and 8-12). The façade of the school included the eight huge arched windows we see today. According to one former long-time middle school Social Studies teacher, the building plan was based upon a design created during Franklin Delano Roosevelt's tenure as Governor of New York State. Built during the Great Depression, a great deal of available labor was used for the construction. Original parts of the building sport foundation walls that are 24 inches thick and there were marble windowsills.

As the district (and the town) was still growing at the time of its completion, there was plenty of extra space for students who lived out of district to attend school there. This practice extended into the 1940s. By the end of the 1940s, students were attending school in double sessions because the population had grown so much.

The 1940s was another pivotal decade in American history. Many high school students left school early to enlist in the Armed Services. Others went right into service after they graduated. But the junior/senior high did even more to support the war movement. Some lucky

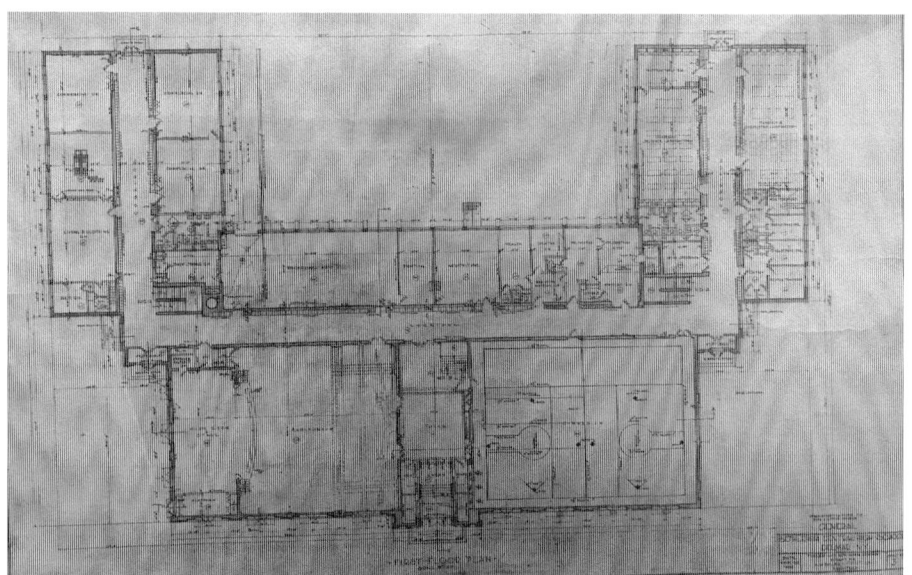

FIGURE 8-11 Original first-floor plan for junior/senior high (courtesy Mr. Michael Klugman, principal, Bethlehem Central Middle School).

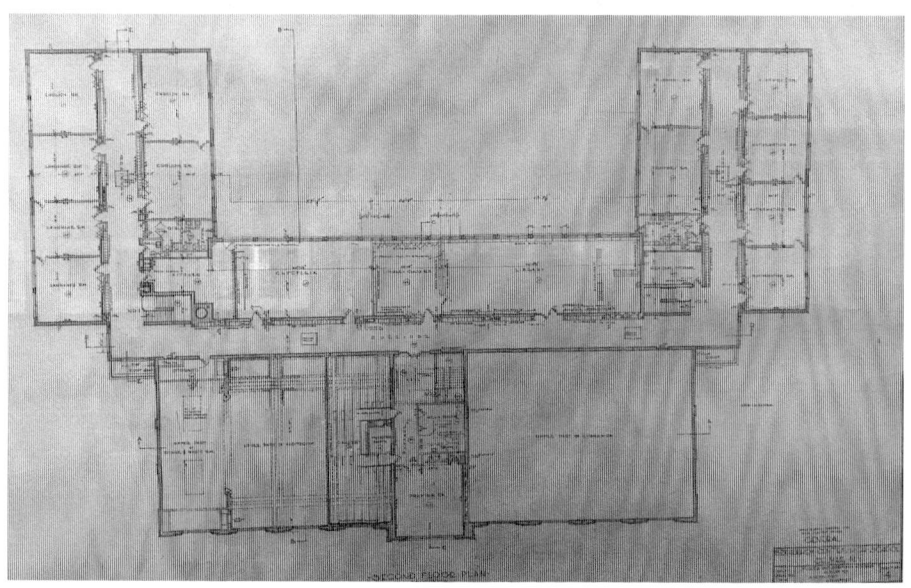

FIGURE 8-12 Original plan for the second floor (courtesy Mr. Michael Klugman, principal, Bethlehem Central Middle School).

Buy War Bonds

WAR BONDS help to support our glider construction course.

When these boys pass this course, they will be eligible to go to the Schweizer Aircraft Plant in Elmira or the American Aircraft Co. in Jamestown as licensed mechanics. The boys have built a working glider as a part of the course.

Picture by Albert I. Howd

The boys who have participated in this course are:

WILLIAM BENNETT	RICHARD BABBITT	CHARLES AGAR
JOHN ALDEN	HARVEY GANTER	WILLIAM SAAR
GRANT VAN PATTEN	VALENTINE WELLS	HENRY JABLONOWSKI
EVERETT CROSSMAN	ROBERT HICKS	KENNETH ELKINTON

EMERSON NEUTHARDT, *Instructor*

FIGURE 8-13 Glider class students and glider (courtesy *Oriole* yearbook).

upperclassmen, in good standing, were trained as plane spotters. They manned a post on the roof and watched for enemy planes.

In the advertising section of the 1943 *Oriole* yearbook, there is an ad for war bonds. It is noted that the sale of war bonds subsidized the glider construction course. Several students are shown in a photo standing next to the glider they built (Figures 8-13 and 8-14). The class was conducted by Mr. Emerson Neuthardt, who came to BC as supervisor of the Industrial Arts Department. He taught at BCHS for five years (1941–1945). Mr. Neuthardt eventually received a Doctorate in Education and taught for over thirty years at SUNY Buffalo.

FIGURE 8-14 Mr. (eventually Doctor) Emerson Neuthardt, originator of Bethlehem Central's glider class (courtesy UBuffalo.edu).

There was a sizable auto shop in the school. It was accessed via a concrete ramp located outdoors in an area roughly behind the original main office. Part of this auto shop was used to house the glider project.

Probably the largest war effort was the sacrifice of many of BC's students in the service of their country. The book *Bethlehem Revisited* (Bethlehem Bicentennial Committee, 1993) contains the names of those who have served in wars throughout our country's history. Too many never returned.

Though the district recruited students from other districts to fill its high school in the late 1930s and early 1940s, population in post-war Bethlehem had increased to the point that the junior/senior high school was in double sessions. Grades 10–12 went to school during the first session and grades 7–9 began their school day at 11:00 a.m. A former student who graduated in the 1950s remembered walking home in the dark from evening choir practice at school. The school continued

FIGURE 8-15 Fallout shelter sign designates the presence of a shelter nearby. These signs were a familiar sight in the 1950s and 1960s.

double sessions, on and off, until the high school on Delaware Avenue was built and occupied in 1954.

Another factor that influenced the schools was the Cold War. The junior/senior high served as a fallout shelter within the community. The recognizable signs were posted and a blast door was put into place in the basement. In the 1960s there was a designated corridor adjacent to the new sixth-grade wing that served as a place to shelter. Sheltering in a sturdy, windowless corridor was preferable to hiding under a desk, though we know now neither measure would have been effective had anything actually happened (Figure 8-15).

Once the new high school building opened in 1954, the school on Kenwood Avenue became a true junior high school housing grades 7–9. There are two murals housed in the school that were painted by the Class of 1957 as a parting gift. They remain in view at the school to this day.

Another important addition to the junior/senior high in 1948 was a vice principal. Mr. William Kinsley was hired to fill the role and to oversee the Guidance Department. Mr. Kinsley was an experienced teacher, having taught in New York City and Long Island. Like Mr. Hamilton Bookhout, Mr. Kinsley was known to put the needs of the children before all else.

Educational trends changed along with the times. By the early 1960s, educators were weighing the differences between a junior high school (grades 7–9) and a middle school (grades 6–8). It was felt that ninth graders were better served when included with the other upper grades. Yet, students going into sixth grade still needed some support

FIGURE 8-16 Proposed additions, circa 1955–1956 (courtesy Mr. Michael Klugman).

as they adjusted to a larger school environment and the need to move to different classrooms throughout the day. Also, the school's physical structure had grown in the late 1950s to keep pace with the increasing population (Figure 8-16).

During the 1960s the concept of a middle school became popular throughout the country. The middle school model was to provide "schools within the school" through team teaching. In this manner, students would be part of a team of about 100 students who had the same teachers for the four main subjects (Math, Social Studies, English, and Science). In addition, other teachers would be assigned to work with the different teams: Second Language, Art, Physical Education, Health, etc. Each student would take classes with the other team members. Therefore, the student's adjustment to a new type of school environment would be done in a supportive and responsible manner.

At this same time, the mid-to-late 1960s, there were substantial increases in the number of students coming through the district. There was room at the senior high school to move the ninth-grade students from the junior high. Many ninth-grade teachers were happy to make the move to the high school, as they had felt isolated being located at the junior high. Many elementary teachers were offered the opportunity to move to the newly designated Bethlehem Central Middle School to teach sixth grade.

The district had to apply to New York State Ed for special certification, as NYS Ed was not keen on the middle school concept in general. Luckily Bethlehem Central had a couple of good models in the area to follow—the Guilderland and Niskayuna School Districts. New Middle School principal Mr. Frederick Burdick, already a veteran teacher and administrator at the high school, worked with the principals of both other schools, and those principals were invited to come and speak with the BC faculty.

Modifications were made to the scheduling to discontinue the bell system and to let teachers pass the students from class to class. Another innovation was to schedule Second Language daily. Subjects like art, music, home economics, and industrial arts were scheduled in 13-week blocks. In this manner, teachers of those subjects saw specific students daily for 13 weeks instead of a staggered schedule where they would see the students only periodically. This benefited the students as well as the teachers.

The middle school model worked well. It allowed teachers a great deal of flexibility in being

FIGURE 8-17 Mr. Frederick Burdick, who oversaw the transition of junior high to middle school. Mr. Burdick was a long-time English teacher at the High School, as well as being a coach and an administrator within the district (courtesy *Oriole* yearbook).

able to work extra time with students. Daily team-teaching meetings also provided the teachers time to plan and implement curriculum with their specific team of students in mind.

From a school standpoint, it was difficult to have ninth graders in the building as their age caused issues with younger children. When BC instituted the middle school concept, both eighth and ninth grades left the school to become part of the high school. It was a move that affected two-thirds of the school population. This changed the entire atmosphere of the newly designated middle school, which was helpful as it created a new opportunity to change behaviors overall. It also enabled an academic focus for teachers and a discipline focus for administrators.

By the late 1960s, the district was helmed by Superintendent Richard Moomaw and assistant superintendent, Dr. Harold Bookbinder. Along with middle school principal Mr. Frederick Burdick (Figure 8-17) and assistant principal Mr. David Murphy, the transition from junior high to middle school was implemented successfully.

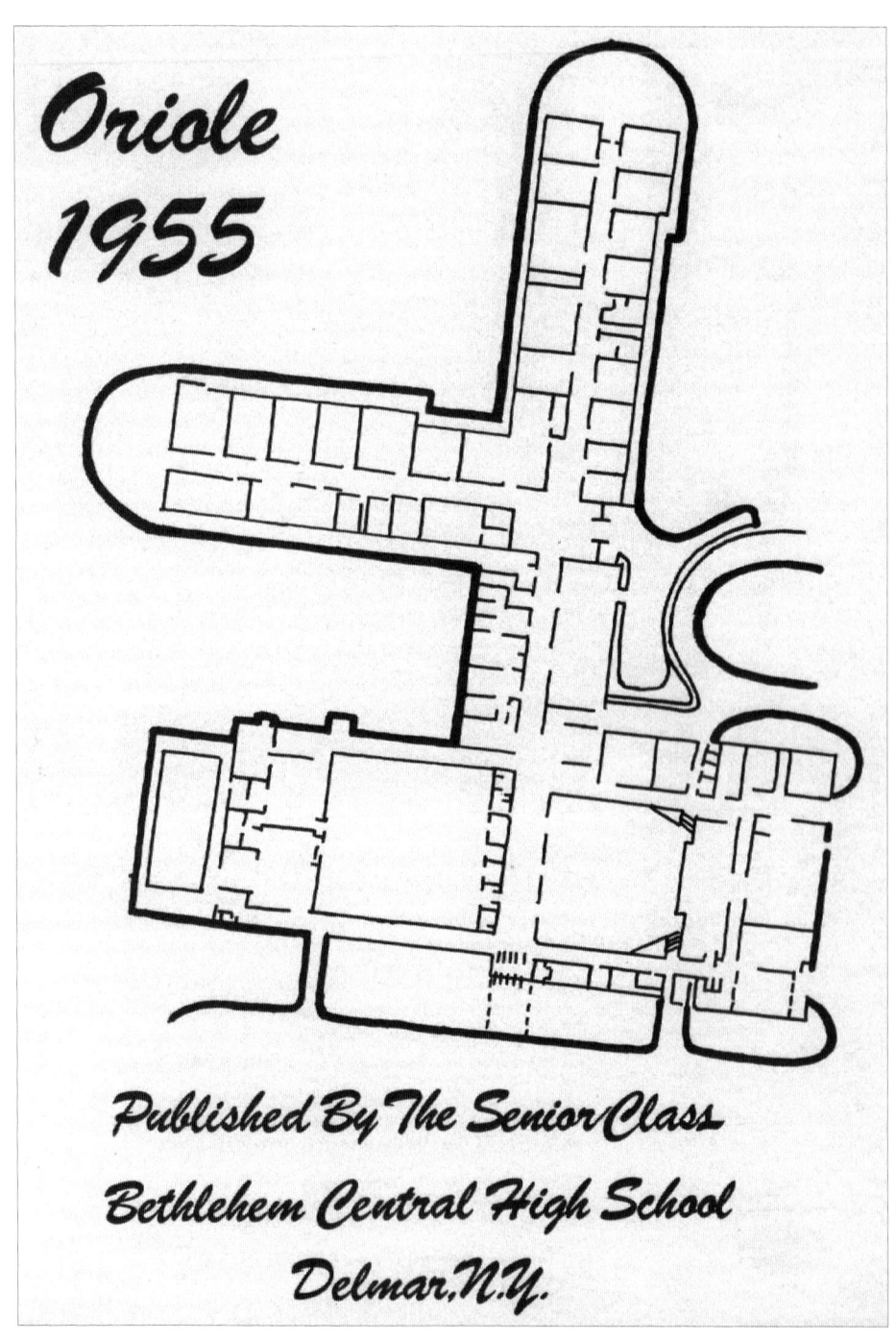

FIGURE 9-1 Original floor plan for the new high school (courtesy *Oriole* yearbook).

CHAPTER 9

700 DELAWARE AVENUE

THE TOWN OF BETHLEHEM continued its growth through the 1940s, especially after the end of World War II. By the late 1940s it was necessary to use double sessions at the junior/senior high. The community knew a new high school was needed, and in 1951 they voted to approve new plans and funding for a new school building. Land that comprised the Stephens farm was purchased. The property adjoined Delaware Avenue and Van Dyke Road. For some perspective, bear in mind that a high school program did not begin until 1926. In less than thirty years, encompassing a nationwide depression and a World War, the school district built three high schools.

The new school opened on January 18, 1954. It was designed to house 450 students in grades 10-12 (Figure 9-1). It carried a price tag of $1.8 million and included 26 classrooms, agriculture and industrial shops, a cafeteria, a library, three music practice rooms, a guidance office, a health office, and supervisory rooms, along with the school and district offices. There was a gymnasium with a capacity of 1,000 people and an auditorium with 900 seats. And there was a swimming pool (Figure 9-2). It must have been exciting to behold a sprawling new school complete with a swimming pool. The only school with a swimming pool at the time was Albany Academy. Just as the building on Kenwood Avenue allowed for increased opportunities for students, so did the new building on Delaware Avenue. The high school welcomed 31 teachers.

FIGURE 9-2 The new pool. Did you ever watch from the balcony? (courtesy *Oriole* yearbook)

An introduction in the 1955 *Oriole* yearbook sums up the excitement for the new senior high school: "...We will find a building functional in every detail. We will see a structure that is beautiful in its own modern way. We will discover gigantic windows, green blackboards, modern furniture, designed as is every part of the building for comfort, health, utility, and pleasure. We will examine a building that was planned to accommodate the needs and wishes of the students. Because of this, the building may be said to be an inanimate manifestation of the students."

Mr. Hamilton Bookhout stepped down as principal of the high school as the new school was constructed. This allowed him to focus on his position as supervising principal (superintendent) of the ever-growing district. On September 11, 1953, the high school welcomed a new principal named Mr. Wilfred Paro (Figure 9-3). He was an experienced educator who had taught in New England and New Jersey. This also began a rotation of principals over the next twenty years in a school that was accustomed to lengthy stays for administrators. Between 1953 and 1973, six principals would helm the high school. These were Mr. Wilfred Paro, Mr. Virgil Tompkins, Mr. Harold Smith, Dr. Kimball Howes, Mr. Paul Runge, and Miss Helen Hobbie, the school's first female principal. Each principal brought unique backgrounds and skill sets to the job which enhanced the atmosphere of the high school.

This was the period of the Cold War. The United States was doing its best to keep in stride with the accomplishments of the Soviet Union. To expand educational opportunities for students, teachers were offered opportunities to enhance their professional skills. These came in the form of grants, fellowships, exchange teaching, and sabbaticals. Many teachers in the district availed themselves of these prospects. A school district with an already exemplary reputation became an even better institution of learning.

One individual who was instrumental in fostering a culture of education among her teachers was Social Studies Supervisor Miss Gladys Newell

FIGURE 9-3 Mr. Wilfred Paro, principal 1954–1956 (courtesy *Oriole* yearbook).

FIGURE 9-4 Miss Gladys Newell (courtesy *Oriole* yearbook).

FIGURE 9-5 Miss Anita Palumbo (courtesy *Oriole* yearbook).

FIGURE 9-6 Mrs. Gladys Hosey (courtesy *Oriole* yearbook).

(Figure 9-4). Miss Newell worked for the district from 1933 to 1971. She was very active in teachers' union activities, especially at the state level. If prospective teachers stopped in the Albany office of the state teachers' union, and they had good credentials, they were directed to the Bethlehem Central School District if there were vacancies. By the same token, any outstanding student teachers coming out of Albany State were directed to Mr. Bookhout or to Miss Newell.

Miss Newell spurred her teachers to continue their educations, and often assigned a historically related book to be read each month and then discussed at monthly department meetings. Miss Newell was present during the growth of the district and was able to increase the quality of curriculum through her encouragement of continuing education for her teachers. It is important to note that Miss Newell was a department supervisor at a time when women were not typically given leadership roles at the secondary level. In fact, the BCSD had two additional female department supervisors. One was Miss Anita Palumbo (eventually Mrs. Cesta), who chaired the Foreign Languages Department. Miss Palumbo began her career at BC in 1946 and left after the 1971–72 school year (Figure 9-5). The third female supervisor was Mrs. Gladys Hosey, who was head of the Business Education Department. Mrs. Hosey (not to be confused with Delmar School's Mrs. Dorothy Hosey) was with the district from 1947 to 1971 (Figure 9-6).

A high academic bar was also set for the students. During the late 1950s, and well into the 1960s and into the 1970s, students were required to do a great number of written assignments in both Social Studies and English. They received intensive instruction in grammar and research methods. Teachers were very expert in the use of our language and were able to correct grammar and mechanics in addition to subject content. For several decades all levels of students were required to write a Social Studies research paper in the eleventh grade (the policies of John Foster Dulles during the Suez Canal Crisis was this writer's assigned topic). These papers had assigned topics and classes were assisted by spending time in the library to receive instruction in the rudiments of research. Students also received this instruction through English class. Papers were required to be typed, properly footnoted, and had to have a bibliography (for more advanced assignments, an annotated bibliography was required). When papers were submitted it was a feeling of great accomplishment for students of all academic levels.

Though standards were high, the students strove to meet them. As the school population increased, so did the opportunities for learning. In the early days of the high school, curriculum was limited to the basic core subjects—English, Math, Civics (Social Studies), and Latin. Choices expanded in the 1930s. This may be seen through the yearbooks over the years in relation to the faculty listings: Commerce (Business), Art, Homemaking, Library, Music, Science, Agriculture, Industrial Arts, and French.

Course offerings increased over time. Throughout the decades, language offerings were consistent with French, Spanish, and Latin. But Chinese, Russian, and German have been taught at different levels as well. The Art Department began to offer photography courses in the late 1960s. Since that time courses have been offered in ceramics, fiber art, sculpture, and video art, to name just a few.

Music is another strong area of curriculum. The early yearbooks portray orchestras consisting of just more than a dozen members, as

FIGURE 9-7

FIGURE 9-8 Mr. Joseph Farrell (courtesy *Oriole* yearbook).

well as choirs of varying sizes. Band uniforms became prominent in the 1940s and lasted through the 1960s (Figure 9-7). There have been quite a variety of smaller instrumental ensembles in addition to larger groups such as Wind Ensemble and Jazz Ensemble. The same is true for vocal groups. Over the decades, BCHS has been consistent in its excellence at statewide evaluations and competitions. Some familiar names in the music department at the high school included Mr. Joseph Farrell, Mr. Sam Bozzella, Mrs. Magdalene York, and Mrs. Santa Ganey, just to name a few (Figures 9-8, 9-9, and 9-10).

Though many fine music instructors worked to create this excellence, the stage was set by Mr. Rolland Truitt. Mr. Truitt was hired by the district in 1936 and retired as the Music Supervisor in 1964 (Figure 9-11). Though not the only music teacher during this period, he was the one who shaped the music program. He was also willing to participate in activities within the community and was an instrumental part of the development of the Delmar Men's Orchestra, an amateur group started in 1940. This group was the subject of a *Life* magazine cover shot and an article called "Amateurs All" in 1955. The cover shot showed the 48 members rehearsing. It is also said that he was influential in helping Eva Marie Saint progress with her career in Hollywood. This offsets the story of the English teacher who, following a tryout for a school play, told Ms. Saint not to pursue theater as she was not suited for it (Figure 9-12). Mr. Truitt lent his talents to many community events, including the very successful Bethlehem White Christmas Festival. The festival began in 1941 and continued for the next few decades until 1969. This event generated funds for the needy. In addition to providing fruit baskets, clothing, and other items, the proceeds from the festival were also used to pay medical and dental bills for children whose families could not pay. An article in *The Spotlight*, dated December 11, 1991, nicely summed up the history of the White Christmas Festival over the years and described why it was no longer held: "The service work of the Bethlehem Festival goes on today, quietly behind the scenes of the holiday hustle and bustle. But

FIGURE 9-9 Mr. Samuel Bozzella (courtesy *Oriole* yearbook).

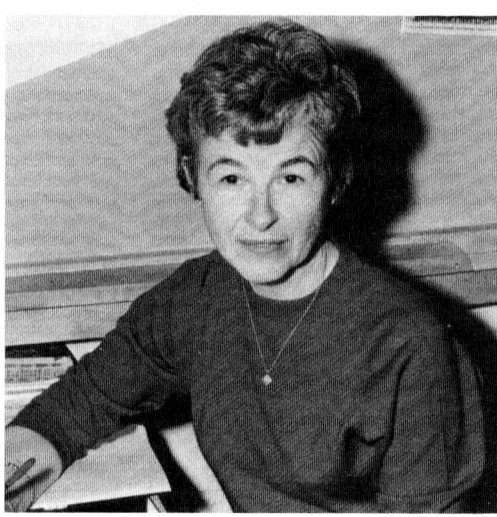

FIGURE 9-10 Mrs. Magdalene York (courtesy *Oriole* yearbook).

FIGURE 9-11 Mr. Rolland Truitt (courtesy *Oriole* yearbook).

the Bethlehem White Christmas is no more, a casualty of changing times and changing sensibilities about what living in a heterogeneous society means."

This was just one of the many changes experienced by the Town of Bethlehem residents, especially after World War II. As already noted, Bethlehem was living proof of the concept of the Protestant Work Ethic. The predominant churches in the town, through the latter part of the nineteenth century and into the dawning of the twentieth century, were the Reformed Church and the Methodist Church. Around 1908, a group of Catholic residents began renting space in a house on the corner of Kenwood and Borthwick Avenues. A priest came out from Albany each Sunday and conducted mass. This was not an unusual practice, as another group (non-Catholic) met in a blacksmith shop on Delaware Avenue until they could afford to build a church. While these are generalizations, they are here because Catholics had a hard time assimilating. However, by the 1950s, the Catholic residents were looking to build a larger church and a school.

The 1950s, supposedly the idyllic decade, also saw the influx of some Jewish families into the town. One individual was recruited by Mr. Hamilton Bookhout to assume an administrative position within the school district. When Mr. Bookhout asked the individual if he and his family had settled into a home, the individual reported

FIGURE 9-12 Eva Marie Saint '42, Academy Award-winning actress who may not have made the cut for the senior play (courtesy *Oriole* yearbook).

FIGURE 9-13 Ms. Miki Cunningham Conn '62 (courtesy Siena.edu).

that no one would show him any houses for sale (the rest of this anecdote was not offered in isolation; it was passed along by several older folks associated with the BCSD). As the story was told, Mr. Bookhout remedied the situation, and the man and his family soon had a residence.

In the latter part of the 1950s a family moved to Delmar from Alaska. The patriarch was a physician who had helped to bridge the gap between Eskimos and Indians and was lauded for that accomplishment. He was so highly esteemed by the native population that he was adopted into the Tlingit tribe. The family thrived in the diverse atmosphere in Alaska and had high hopes for life in Delmar because the town was so highly recommended, mainly due to the lauded academic program.

The reception was far from what the family expected. Even though the town was full of a variety of professional people, many residents made it known they were not keen on an African American family moving into the neighborhood. Ms. Miki Cunningham Conn arrived in Delmar just in time to begin junior high (Figure 9-13). Ms. Conn said people's treatment of them was mostly passive. People avoided them and did not make eye contact. The kids in the neighborhood were willing to play with her and her younger sister if their parents did not find out.

Ms. Conn was hard pressed to recall any teachers' names because they did not pay much attention to her as a student. She did say her seventh- and eighth-grade English teachers were accepting of her. They recognized her intellect and ability and tried to bolster her courage in various ways. Ms. Conn recalls envying the easy relationships the other kids had with one another. On a positive note, Ms. Conn said she could be herself because she had no competition. Her lack of being included resulted in a deeper interest in reading and nature. Both are still important parts of Ms. Conn's life. After graduation in June 1962,

FIGURE 9-14 Mr. Herman Brown (courtesy *Oriole* yearbook).

she went off to Howard University and never returned to Delmar. Her parents and younger sister moved to Schenectady.

Perhaps the ultimate manifestation of this type of discomfort came in the early spring of 1969. A six-part lecture series entitled "Black History and Culture" was to begin in the evenings at BCHS. A student-sponsored event, to which the Bethlehem Central Teacher's Association contributed funding, was abruptly canceled. Three of the high school social studies teachers had even gone out of their way to procure the speakers. In a *Knickerbocker News* article dated April 3, 1969, entitled, "'Pressure' in Bethlehem Ends Black History Culture Series," it was reported that high school teacher Mr. Herman Brown received a variety of threats via telephone merely because he was a BCTA representative who had advocated for the lecture series (Figure 9-14). Though the initial lecture series was canceled, the speakers (Leon Van Dyke and the Brothers) did appear in a different type of forum.

As the volatile decade of the 1960s ended, change was still in the air. The teachers in the BCSD had a labor affiliation with state and national level teachers' unions. It was not until this time that the local teacher's union, the Bethlehem Central Teacher's Association, began to make a name for itself. The BC teachers had been working without a contract for quite a while. The local union began to strengthen and unify in its quest for a reasonable contract. The BCSD was not the only district in this situation at the time. Ballston Spa and Schenectady lacked contracts as did a handful of other communities in New York State.

In March 1969, a mediator was appointed to settle the impasse between the Bethlehem Central Teacher's Association (BCTA) and the Board of Education (BOE). The primary issues at stake were 1) the salary schedules for teachers, supervisors, and principals, and 2) an additional month of employment for supervisors. The two parties could not agree. With the 1970–71 school year approaching, the teachers still did not have a contract. It was decided the teachers would picket before and after school. They would honor the school day and it would not interfere with student education. The BCTA considered picketing as informational, and the intention was for it not to prevent students from crossing the picket lines.

The BCTA was fighting for its teachers to receive an equitable salary, extra duty pay, and health insurance, among other issues. In a September 20, 1970, *Knickerbocker News* "Letter to the Editor," a former BC teacher wrote, "I couldn't help but feel the personal degradation of the teachers when I drove my son, who will be a junior, to the senior high school. He had been chosen to guide the new freshmen through

FIGURE 9-15 Bethlehem Central Teacher's Association (BCTA) on strike. Mr. Ralph Brown and Mr. Rick Poplaski, high school Social Studies teachers, hold picket signs (courtesy Facebook).

FIGURE 9-16 BCTA teachers picketing in front of Elsmere School (note Mullens Pharmacy in the background). Teachers facing the camera, l. to r.: Mr. Al Restifo (MS), Mr. Anthony Bango (HS), Miss Karen Rothaupt (HS), Mrs. Connie Jensen (HS), and Mrs. Tona Riggio (HS) (courtesy Facebook).

the school on their day of orientation. He was proud! As a former BC teacher, I wanted to weep. I left a few years ago, after many years of service to that school system, for the same reasons they are marching now: Working Conditions." These are strong and heartfelt words from a former colleague and parent of a student.

The BCTA had voted to call a strike if no new offers were made from the BOE. Though the teachers had been picketing each day that week, they were also fulfilling their duties as teachers. On Thursday night of the opening week of school, Mr. Warren Stoker, the President of the BCTA, made the call to strike. Friday morning, September 11, 1970, teachers were picketing and on strike (Figures 9-15 and 9-16). Of the district's 292 teachers, 49 reported for work on that Friday. Clarksville and Glenmont schools had full days of school.

One prominent non-striker was Social Studies supervisor Miss Gladys Newell. Miss Newell felt she was free to cross the picket line because the strike was illegal, and her conscience would not allow her to strike. She had helped to found the BCTA and she told them she supported them fully up to striking and it did not mean her sympathies were not with the teachers.

A court order was issued for the teachers to resume work and negotiations between the BCTA and BOE resumed that Saturday. The BCTA, satisfied that negotiations had resumed, voted to return to work on Monday. In the interim, most of the teachers were served subpoenas (one while in the shower). Striking was against the law, and they could have gone to jail. This must have been daunting to the 26 newly hired teachers that year. The BCTA was coming together to become a strong organization for its teachers. Their claim for the stalemate was the lack of a negotiated contract for its teachers. They were also seeking binding arbitration, which already existed in the North and South Colonie districts.

Sparks would fly again in February 1971 when the BCSD hired a new superintendent (at an annual salary of $28,000) without any say or input from the BCTA. The BCTA increased their demands for decision-making involvement. The BOE felt the BCTA interviewers would not maintain confidentiality.

Over the years the BCTA has represented its constituents admirably. It is a significant part of decision-making processes across the district. While contract negotiations have been tense at times and work-to-rule conditions have been followed, there has yet to be another work stoppage since the one-day strike in 1970.

Another aspect that has continually evolved is curriculum. During the 1960s and 70s, some of the core disciplines expanded their curricula by offering elective classes to the students. Electives are courses that usually last one semester in length. They were taken in addition to any core courses, and not intended as a replacement for core courses. In this manner, students were able to explore some subject areas in greater depth. For example, social studies for juniors was a year-long American History class. One would take American History but could opt to take one of the offered electives as well (e.g., psychology, sociology, etc.). There were electives in English and Science as well. Electives were able to capitalize on teachers' interests and specialty areas. Though all teachers in New York State must be permanently certified and have received a master's degree, teachers are individuals who have unique interests and experiences.

It was previously mentioned that the Social Studies Department was encouraged to take advantage of travel and study opportunities. As a result, there were courses offered in such subjects as Middle Eastern history, Asian history, and Canadian history; these are a small tip of an enormous iceberg.

The English Department offered electives such as Detective Fiction, Novel of Social Protest, Theater Arts, and American Musical Theater, to name a few. Science had electives such as Wildlife Biology and Ecology.

It is not possible to list every elective that was offered and taught. They represented a wide range of interests and expertise. Students have benefitted for decades because they have had these courses to enjoy.

Town population and class sizes continued to increase. A bond issue in the late 1950s accommodated additions at several of the district schools. The high school, which opened with 88,840 square feet, added another 40,000 square feet. It was amazing that a school that had been open for just six years needed so much more space.

This was nothing compared to the two-story wing and additional gymnasium that were added in 1968 (Figure 9-17). These changes resulted in the addition of 127,624 square feet of space to the school. It was around this same time that the junior high became a middle school housing grades 6–8 and the senior high became a true high school housing grades 9–12. Ninth-grade teachers were given the opportunity to move to the high school. Many did and were pleased to become part of the high school community.

Educational opportunities have continued to expand through the ensuing decades. A robust Advanced Placement program allows students to graduate from high school with college credits resulting from passage of a variety of Advanced Placement classes. Students may take a series of

FIGURE 9-17 Lower gym, aka the Boys Gym aka Gym B, after flooding caused the floor to warp (courtesy *Oriole* yearbook).

courses designed for engineering. There are electives pertaining to child development and child psychology. These could be important to a student considering teaching as a profession. Any student contemplating culinary arts has a handful of courses from which to choose.

Graduates from BCHS have a high rate (over 90 percent) of further education, whether in 2-year or 4-year institutions. Students are well prepared for the academic demands of higher learning. BCHS is consistently ranked highly on both local and national levels. In the most recent rankings from *US News and World Report* (April 2022), BCHS is "ranked #1 in the region, #84 in New York State, and #795 in the nation." The latter figure is an improvement from #901 the previous year. The district's founders would be proud.

At some point in time the tradition of naming a valedictorian and salutatorian ceased. Information regarding this decision was unable to be found. A wise woman, valedictorian of the Class of 1944, said she attended Syracuse University for one year and decided it wasn't for her. She asked her father for a loan and moved to New York City, where she

FIGURE 9-18 1929 HS faculty. Delmar High celebrated its first graduating class. Standing: Mr. Stephen Prokop (math and science), Mr. Olin Bouck, principal. Seated: Miss Mildred Currie (French and math), Miss Helen Knowles (Latin), Miss Lillian Rexford (English), Miss Violet Smith (music and art). Missing: Miss Roslyn Chapman (history and coach of girls' basketball). Note the pillars on the façade of Delmar High, still visible at the entrance of the current Town Hall (courtesy *Oriole* yearbook).

immediately found a job. It would lead to an opportunity to travel to Ecuador, where she met a Canadian engineer whom she later married. They spent 64 years together. She was widely criticized for giving up her scholarship to take a clerical job. After all, she was the valedictorian. One might say she made a good choice.

Many good choices over the decades have allowed the Bethlehem Central School District to be consistently ranked among, or, at, the top of the list for the schools in the Capital District. When, in 1907, the residents of the town thought they had built the last school that would be needed, they were not able to envision a bridge improvement would bring so many residents to settle in the Town of Bethlehem. Delmar High, which started with a faculty of just seven and an initial graduating class of thirteen students (Figures 9-18 and 9-19), has grown into a high school that employs 160+ faculty, has graduated classes of 300–500 in the last several decades, and is consistently ranked a top school in the area; this record undoubtedly shows an evolution to excellence, backed by the foundation provided by the elementary schools and the middle school.

FIGURE 9-19 Original yearbook emblem. Façade pictured is the building on the corner of Delaware and Borthwick Avenues. This high school became Delmar Elementary school and then, in 1980, the Bethlehem Town Hall (courtesy *Oriole* yearbook).

FIGURE 10-1 Delmar Train Station (courtesy Town of Bethlehem via Leonard Welter).

FIGURE 10-2 Delmar High School Baseball team, 1930 (courtesy *Oriole* yearbook).

CHAPTER 10

STUDENT LIFE

To say that life was different in the Town of Bethlehem almost 100 years ago would be an understatement. Delmar was a sleepy outpost of Albany, which was readily accessible by train, but roads to and from the city were few, rustic, and not very safe. Prior to 1926, when a high school program was first offered, Bethlehem students often took the train to Albany or to Ravena to attend high school (Figure 10-1). On nice days some students rode their bicycles into Albany to attend school. By the same token, many students from Voorheesville took the train to Delmar to attend school.

When the high school program began in 1926, radio and film were just becoming commonplace. Most families at the time were used to entertaining within the home, and at gatherings with friends and neighbors. Many people played musical instruments and sang. Plays and concerts were featured at local churches until larger school buildings were built.

Newspapers from the first twenty years of the twentieth century also featured many articles of baseball results. It seemed as though each small town fielded a team that travelled to other areas to play games. This attests to the popularity of the game and its importance in the leisure time of people in the early 1900s. Fielding a baseball team at the high school would be a challenge in the early years due to the small number of students enrolled. There were boys' and girls' basketball teams from the beginning and often a baseball team (Figure 10-2).

FIGURE 10-3 For decades, Saturday afternoons meant football games played behind the junior/senior high/middle school (courtesy *Oriole* yearbook).

FIGURE 10-4 The junior high before the cafeteria addition (courtesy *Oriole* yearbook).

As the years went by and the student population increased, football became a staple sport. But instead of using teams of eleven men each, it was played using six-man teams well into the early 1940s. Soccer was fielded off and on over the years. The school facility, from its inception, had a cinder track that contained a football field within its perimeter. Saturday afternoon football games reigned, and each glorious fall season supporters trooped to the bleachers behind the school building on Kenwood Avenue to cheer on their team. This tradition lasted until the late 1980s when games were moved to the Delaware Avenue site and lights were installed. Games were then played on Friday nights (Figures 10-3, 10-4, and 10-5).

Tennis was a popular activity and was played on the two courts behind the junior/senior high school building on Kenwood Avenue. No

FIGURE 10-5 Football bleachers behind the junior/senior high (courtesy *Oriole* yearbook).

FIGURE 10-6 Coach Don Camp and his 1948 basketball team. In 1950 Coach Camp was named the area's basketball coach of the year (courtesy *Oriole* yearbook).

mention of tennis would be complete without a word about Mr. Don Camp: Mr. Camp was a memorable English teacher at BCHS from 1946 to 1978, but he may be best remembered as a terrific and successful coach. Many memories are associated with his long tenure as the boys' varsity tennis coach, but in the late 1940s and very early 1950s, Mr. Camp also coached boys' basketball and in 1950 was named Coach of the Year. Also an excellent bowler, Mr. Camp's true sport was tennis. He excelled both on a personal level in tournaments and as a coach, and his efforts to provide a summer tennis instruction program for children resulted in a keen interest in tennis for hundreds of children over the years. In addition, in the mid-1960s, Mr. Camp helped to organize the Bethlehem Tennis Association, a community-based organization that organized tournaments and instruction for a few decades.

During the 1960s and early 1970s, the BCHS Varsity Boys' Tennis Team, under Mr. Camp's guidance, compiled a streak of 90 consecutive wins that, after being broken by a single loss to rival Niskayuna on May 11, 1971, was followed by another streak of 30 consecutive wins. Tennis remains a strongly contested sport at BCHS, with both girls' and boys' teams maintaining a strong presence among local teams (Figures 10-6 and 10-7).

FIGURE 10-7 Coach Don Camp and a tennis team from the 1960s. (Photo courtesy *Oriole* yearbook; Information courtesy *Knickerbocker News*).

Early yearbooks show a rickety-looking orchestra, though it seems they played with enthusiasm. With the district's knack for securing excellent teachers, Mr. Rolland Truitt was hired to head up the music program and taught in the district from 1936 to 1964. He emerged as a *tour de force* who shaped the music department during his tenure. He oversaw both instrumental and vocal aspects of the music department for many years (Figure 10-8).

Music eventually became part of the curriculum, though there were many ensembles and singing groups that were popular after-school activities. The first few decades also saw students who had their own bands or combos that hired themselves out for dances and parties. As times changed, these evolved into rock bands instead of orchestras.

FIGURE 10-8 Mr. Rolland Truitt (courtesy *Oriole* yearbook).

Students using their own bands to entertain at student-based functions

> Compliments of
>
> **JOHNNY HAUF and HIS ORCHESTRA**
>
> Open for Engagements
>
> Dial 9-898

FIGURE 10-9 Student band advertisement in an *Oriole* yearbook from the 1930s. A three-number telephone number indicates an early Delmar resident. The Delmar telephone exchange was Hemlock or HE9 (439) or just 9. This system of telephone exchanges was discontinued in the 1960s.

have enjoyed a long tradition at BCHS. Dances were held during the 1920s and continue to be held this day. Prior to the opening of the larger high school building on Kenwood Avenue in 1934, many dances were held in the Delmar or Elsmere Schools due to their larger size. Each school featured an auditorium/gymnasium, and each had a stage to feature the musicians, and there was plenty of floor space for dancing. Dances were announced in the local newspapers. It is unclear whether the dances were open to students from outside the local school district (Figure 10-9).

Another form of student entertainment was the Delmar Theatre, which began showing movies in 1929. The theatre was located at 333 Delaware Avenue and was a local student hangout. Many teenagers fondly referred to the theatre as "the Dump" while others called it "the Stink" (Figure 10-10). A 1956 BCHS graduate explained that Friday nights were for checking out students of the opposite sex as possible date bait. Saturday nights were for serious dating. The Delmar Theatre remained open until 1959.

The idea for a youth center began as early as the mid-1940s. A newspaper article published in 1947 reported a committee of "church, civic, and school leaders" threw their support behind the idea. Students in-

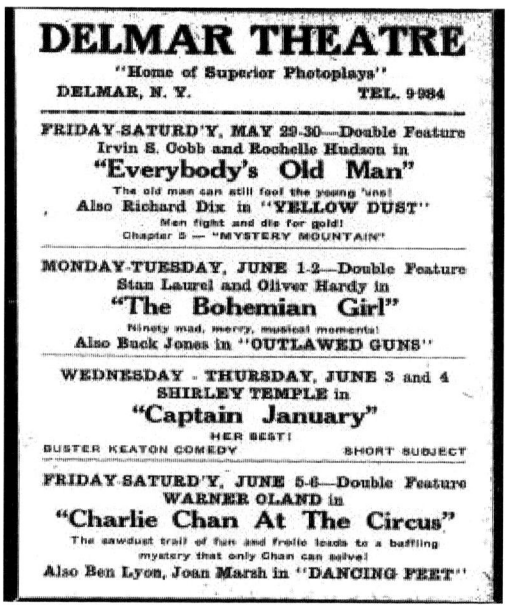

FIGURE 10-10 An ad for The Delmar Theatre, aka The Stink, which was located at 333 Delaware Avenue for three decades (courtesy *Altamont Enterprise*).

volved in the campaign were members of the Girls Hi-Y chapter in the high school.

Hi-Y was a social club affiliated with the YMCA and YWCA organizations. Its purpose was "to create, maintain, and extend, throughout the home, school, and community, high standards of Christian character." There were separate clubs for boys and girls. BCHS had both. The girl's chapter was called the Carlson Chapter of the Tri Hi-Y and the boy's chapter was known as the David Knapp Chapter of the Tri Hi-Y (further research showed that David Knapp attended BCHS through his junior year and then entered the United States Navy. David is listed by the U.S. Defense POW/MIA Accounting Agency under Unaccounted-for-Remains, Group B (Unrecoverable), 1941–1975. His death date is given as August 9, 1942, in the Solomon Islands (Figures 10-11 and 10-12).

The 1947 newspaper article discussed the difficulty in finding a location for the youth center, but the center was tentatively scheduled to open that summer. Apparently, a solution was never reached as there is no further mention of a youth center until 1952.

In 1952, the youth center became a certainty. A public meeting was held to enlist the support of residents. More than 150 of the townspeople were in attendance. At the meeting was Mr. John Lutzen, of the New York State Youth Commission, who addressed the need for a "broad program under trained leadership." The Bethlehem Central Board of Education made available the amount of $3500 for a new recre-

FIGURE 10-11 The Carlson Chapter (Girls) of Tri Hi-Y (courtesy *Oriole* yearbook).

FIGURE 10-12 The Knapp Chapter (Boys) of Tri Hi-Y (courtesy *Oriole* yearbook).

FIGURE 10-13 Mr. Richard Rugg was hired in the 1950s to teach and to run the new Student Canteen, also known as The Pit (courtesy *Oriole* yearbook).

ation director at BCHS. The new faculty member's duties would include teaching as well as directing the activities of the youth center. Students pledged to paint and paper whatever site was chosen. They also promised to distribute literature about the youth center during the funding drive. An adult advisory board was appointed to search for a site.

The advisory board located a property on Delaware Avenue that was deemed appropriate. It had belonged to the Rivkin family and had been made available when they moved from Delmar. The sale of the property, referred to as "the Rivkin estate," in newspaper articles, was set to proceed until it was learned the property had a 50-year restriction on it. The restriction stipulated that if the property was sold, it had to remain a residential property for a period of 50 years.

After a two-year study of locations, it was determined a large space under the original gymnasium at the then BC Junior High School, on Kenwood Avenue, would be modified and utilized. Digging would be required to lower the floor level, though parents were assured the youth center would not be below ground level. Lighting, ventilation, painting, and floor installation would cost approximately $11,500. Local builder Mr. Harold Geurtze did the construction. Over $8,000 was raised through the combined efforts of the Adult Advisory Committee and the BCHS Youth Council. Mr. Richard Rugg, a SUNY Cortland graduate, was hired in 1953 as the new recreation director for the high school. His job also included the supervision of five playgrounds during the summer (Figure 10-13).

The youth center, also known as the canteen in its early days, became self-supporting. There was a dedicated Canteen Council at BCHS,

Canteen Show Hits the Boards

annual production... profits used to improve the Canteen... "Maybe this year we could sound-proof it"... show's M.C. always a vital factor... "And now for my next joke"... senior girls give it their annual try... "Oh well, if at first you don't succeed..."

The senior girls' annual try.

FIGURE 10-14 A canteen show was held annually by the Canteen Council. It was a student-driven talent show. Proceeds helped to fund the canteen (courtesy *Oriole* yearbook).

THE DELMAR CANTEEN has become the center of pleasant, wholesome life for teenagers of the Town of Bethlehem.

FIGURE 10-15 A scene from the Canteen (courtesy Rudy Zwicklbauer '63).

and among fundraising activities was the Canteen Show (Figure 10-14). This event showcased student acts of various types and was popular through the 1960s. Money raised was used for furniture, games, music, and snacks.

Many former teenagers, no matter the decade they attended BCHS, can recall various memories of activities at "the Pit," as it came to be known. From dances (during the summer) to ice skating (each of these activities took place on the tennis courts), to music, and games, the Pit was the place to be (Figure 10-15). Gatherings were especially popular after football and basketball games. If you happen to encounter an alumnus of BCHS, ask him or her about the Pit. You're sure to hear some sort of tale!

Town of Bethlehem children also engaged in activities that have been popular for centuries, namely skating and sledding. An article from *The Altamont Enterprise*, dated January 27, 1922, recounts a sleigh-ride party on a Wednesday afternoon that included the boys from grades 2–6. All the boys then had supper at the Austin home on Kenwood Avenue. Historical records point to two young men, Erwin Austin (who went on to become a noted artist and designer) and his brother Richard. Erwin graduated in the second high school class in Delmar in 1930 and Richard graduated in 1932. The brothers lived with their parents on Kenwood Avenue. What a fun time for all those boys!

Opportunities for sledding and skating were abundant throughout the town. Skating parties on the large pond located on Delaware Avenue (formerly the Wynkoop property) were advertised in *The Altamont Enterprise* during the 1920s. Smaller ponds—such as Herrick's Pond on McCormack Road in Slingerlands and VonRonne's Pond at the end of Hudson Avenue—were located throughout the town. According to a graduate of the class of 1940 who lived on Adams Place, there was a pond on the opposite side of Roweland Avenue that was not only used for ice skating, but residents also cut ice from it! During the 1950s and 1960s, an area at Glenmont School was flooded to make a skating rink. After the Town Park was opened in the mid-1970s, a large area was flooded to make a rink. It was large enough for pick-up ice hockey games.

> EIGHT MODERN BRUNSWICK
> **BOWLING ALLEYS**
> and the Finest ROLLER SKATING RINK in the Capital District
> **SPORTHAVEN**
> 419 Kenwood Ave. DELMAR Telephone 9-1110

FIGURE 10-16 Advertisement in the Tri-Village Directory (aka the Snoop Book, Nosy Book, Bible) for Sporthaven Lanes in Delmar. By the mid-1960s, Del Lanes was built and made Delmar a two-bowling-alley town (courtesy *Tri-Village Directory*).

Sledding required a hill, and for smaller children even a tiny hill would do. Normanside Country Club provided many large hills for children to experience an exciting sledding outing. A small hill adjacent to Doctor Harold Browne's house on Delaware Avenue provided many neighborhood children the opportunity for fun. A fringe benefit was that Doctor Browne was handy to tend to any sledding injuries. It's a guarantee there were many more locations for winter fun throughout the town.

The town of Delmar even had a bowling alley early on. It was called Sporthaven Lanes and it was located on the corner of Kenwood Avenue and Adams Street (Figure 10-16). The lower floor contained a roller rink and the upper floor contained bowling lanes. Many a skating party took place there, as did recreational and league bowling. In the 1960s another bowling alley was constructed in Delmar closer to the border of Delmar and Albany. Roughly across from Delaware Plaza, it was called Del Lanes. It is still in operation today.

The first fifty years of the school district featured an active Greek life among members of the high school. Evidence of this goes all the way back to an advertisement in the inaugural yearbook of 1929 for a sorority named Delta Psi. The following year featured a fraternity named Sigma Kappa Delta that continued for many decades. Another long-lived fraternity was Phi Delta Phi. Others included Tau Epsilon Psi and TKB (Tappa Kega Beer). Long-lived sororities were Beta Gamma Rho and Sigma Theta Epsilon. Some others were Delta Psi and Gamma Rho (Figures 10-17 and 10-18).

FIGURE 10-17 A medley of fraternity jackets, l. to r.: Tau Epsilon Psi (brown/gold), Phi Delta Phi (green/white), Sigma Kappa Delta (black/gold) (courtesy *Oriole* yearbook).

It would seem this high school Greek life mimicked that of college. Ironically, five of the ten oldest fraternities began at Union College. One fraternity, Alpha Zeta, was the first high school fraternity in 1869 at Union Classical Institute, a secondary school affiliated with Union College. High school Greek life, as it existed at BCHS, was a social experience. Sororities often held dances and went to sorority camp each summer. There are newspaper articles telling of Sigma Kappa Delta's experiences collecting for the March of Dimes, mainly in the 1950s. Also in the 1950s, the patriarch of a young Delmar family was stricken with polio. The sisters of Beta Gamma Rho organized themselves to babysit, prepare meals, and help the family.

Sigma Kappa Delta appeared in another newspaper article in 1953. A local resident had given the group access to an old shed, off Hudson Avenue, to use as a clubhouse. Apparently, the gatherings became consistently noisy and disruptive. The property owner took them to court, and they were evicted. At least one other fraternity, Phi Delta Phi, in the 1950s was given access to a shed that served as a clubhouse. This one was reported to be in the woods quite a distance

FIGURE 10-18 Jacket for Tappa Kega Beer (courtesy John C. Bohl Jr. '76).

FIGURE 10-19 Mr. Glenn Wagner's headstone reflects his passion for Boy Scouts and model railroading (courtesy Findagrave.com).

behind the Tollgate in Slingerlands. It is unclear if these organizations were ever fully sanctioned by the school. If any still exist, they are underground organizations.

Outside of school, another tradition children have enjoyed in the Town of Bethlehem is Boy Scouts, Girl Scouts, and 4-H. Scout packs and troops often grew out of the individual elementary schools. All experienced various rates of growth and demise. The Boy Scouts were lucky to have Glenn Wagner, a prolific writer and editor for *Boys' Life*, the national magazine for Boy Scouts, living in Delmar for a few decades (Figure 10-19). Former Boy Scouts from the 1950s and 1960s remarked they were often used to test the various experiments and activities Mr. Wagner developed as articles for the magazine. Mr. Wagner would photograph the boys as they built or created the various projects (Figure 10-20). What a nice incentive to see a photo of oneself in a national magazine!

Research uncovers important information, and it also uncovers some very amusing information. Here is a fun story. In July 1964, a group of neighborhood boys thought up a wholesome activity to pass the time. The *Times Union* story, published on July 16, 1964, credits Doug Chesser with the idea of bicycling around the block for 24 straight hours (Figure 10-21). He and his friends set out on a Friday at 6:00 p.m. They had a plan for how many laps each rider would ride consecutively before passing off to the next rider. Since they wanted the bicycle to keep moving, they changed riders "pony express" style, with both boys running alongside the bike. Tom Harris, Harold Hasselbarth, Jack Fairbank, Tom

FIGURE 10-20 Boy Scouts Dick Owen '63 and Tom Wilson '65 use a racetrack made by Glenn Wagner in this photograph, which was taken by Wagner in his basement and later appeared in *Boys' Life* magazine in 1962.

FIGURE 10-21 A wholesome activity for summer vacation (courtesy Doug Chesser '66 via the *Albany Times Union*).

Hasselbarth, and Doug Chesser kept the bicycle going for 24 hours. They even claimed they did not coast at all, pedaling the entire time. It was an inventive way to pass the time during summer vacation.

Take a minute to think about social customs during the 1940s–1980s. Protocol related to dating required boys to ask girls on dates, as was the tradition. However, at least one dance a year allowed the girls to turn the tables. The dance was called the Daisy Mae Drag and was a fundraiser for each junior class. This type of dance was known as a Sadie Hawkins Dance. History tells us the tradition came from Al Capp's popular comic strip *Li'l Abner.* The characters of the comic strip lived in the village of Dogpatch. Each November, on an unspecified date, the character of Sadie Hawkins would encourage all of the unmarried women in Dogpatch to chase the bachelors and "marry up." Thus, the Daisy Mae Drag at BCHS took place in late October or early November. Often there was a skit featuring students playing

FIGURE 10-22 An early example of students dressed for the annual Daisy Mae Drag skit. The dance was held in the fall (courtesy *Oriole* yearbook).

Dogpatch characters. But the best part was the girls were able to ask the boys to the dance. The earliest mention of this dance was 1946 and it continued into the 1980s. Also, if a Sadie Hawkins Dance was held during the winter, it was called a Snow Ball. BCHS had these dances as well (Figure 10-22).

Another fun activity, to celebrate Homecoming in the fall, was the pep rally. The activities making up the pep rally have changed over the decades, but the common denominators—football, fall, enthusiasm, and competition—remain the same. At one point in time during the 1950s students would have a parade of sorts, beginning at the old junior high on Kenwood Avenue. It wound its way over Oakwood Place to Delaware Avenue, where the cheering parade members gained support

Coach and captains throw Columbia in the fire at the Pep Rally.

FIGURE 10-23 The traditional bonfire at the annual Pep Rally (courtesy *Oriole* yearbook).

from the honking of passing cars. Another favorite activity in conjunction with the Pep Rally was the bonfire. A large bonfire was constructed on the school property to be enjoyed the night before the game. Both activities were discontinued long ago (Figure 10-23).

Left for us to ponder are the following: the design of the school crest, the name of *Oriole* used for the yearbook, and the choice of the eagle as the school's mascot. One might ask about the school's alma mater. The words were written by Alfred Marston '36; his mother, Mrs. Elizabeth Marston, was a longtime Art teacher during the district's first few decades. The music was borrowed from Cornell University's alma mater. A newer musical arrangement appeared in the 1960s, written by Thomas Scurrah '68. Many former students remember learning this song during their school days.

FIGURE 10-24 The title page from the first *Oriole* yearbook (courtesy *Oriole* yearbook).

The yearbook has always been known as the *Oriole* (Figure 10-24). Those who may have known why have passed long ago. One story refers to a few high school students lounging on the grass outside of Delmar High. One student spotted an oriole, and the rest is history. Could it be that simple? We will likely never know. The school colors orange and black coincide with the oriole concept. But we are the Bethlehem Eagles, not the Orioles. Speculation is the eagle has a fiercer connotation than an oriole. Again, we may never know.

If one purchased a school ring, one may know the school crest appears on it. The crest is composed of a handful of images that draw from local history and from academic tradition. There is a Latin motto, "Quanti Sapere Est," or "how valuable (great) is wisdom." Three symbols on the crest relate to academics. The open book represents the free sharing of knowledge. At its simplest level, the torch symbolizes knowledge and/or enlightenment. The symbol of the lamp is representative of the traditional Lamp of Learning. Relating to our local history is the image of the *Half Moon*, Henry Hudson's flagship, and the image of a native American, the people indigenous to this area. If one still has a class ring, the crest is now decoded (Figure 10-25).

By no means are these all the activities that have been available to students over the years. This is the very tip of an enormous iceberg. This one small chapter could be turned into its own book, complete with many pictures. It would be its own time capsule. The premise of the book was to discover and explain how the Bethlehem Central

> ## The Emblem
>
>
> Our school emblem, symbolic of local history and scholarly attributes, was the winning entry for the best original design of a school emblem in a contest held for Bethlehem Central students in the 1930's.
>
> The ship is Hendrick Hudson's "Half Moon," and the Indian represents those who met early European immigrants.
>
> The motto, "Of what great value it is to know," found on the emblem, is illustrated by the open book, symbolizing available learning; by the lamp, representing personal wisdom, knowledge, and intellect; and by the torch, expressing the individual's responsibility to pass on the learning and ideals which he has been taught.

FIGURE 10-25 An explanation of the school emblem from the 1950 *Oriole* (courtesy *Oriole* yearbook).

School District created such an excellent academic program in a relatively short time. Space and time did not allow for discussion of so many other topics. The excellent theater program, enhanced and expanded by Mr. Richard Feldman, deserves a book of its own. Loads of sports teams were not discussed, including the swimming empire, managed over many decades, by Mr. Clarence Lephart, Mr. Ray Sliter, Mr. Jack Whipple, and Mr. Ken Neff. And there is no discussion of how the girls' athletic teams grew in leaps and bounds after Title IX in the early 1970s.

It is so important to preserve this history. Perhaps others will be inspired to seek out some individuals to get their take on the many topics mentioned. At the very least, the information could be preserved in our public library's local history files.

AFTERWORD

THIS JOURNEY TOOK ME FAR AND WIDE. It began with a simple question: How did our local school district have such a great reputation by the 1940s when its high school program began in 1926? This question popped into my head while researching an article I was writing for the Bethlehem Historical Association newsletter. I needed some very specific information about an experimental high school housed in Delmar in 1917. The more I dug, the less information I found. A huge hole existed regarding the early years of the school district.

The idea of a project took shape in my head. I'd combine facts, anecdotal information derived from personal interviews, and photographs into a book on the first fifty years of the district. I'd also make sure students were involved in the project as well. Sounds easy, doesn't it? Several years later, the project has come as far as I am able to bring it. It is not complete by any stretch of the imagination, but additional work is for others to do. Someone needs to capture the story of the development of the theater program, for example.

Many, many old newspaper articles have been read. Many, many people have given of their time and spoken with me. Many, many hours were devoted to research. I shamelessly asked for information through social media sources. I sat, early on, for an interview with a reporter from our local *Spotlight* newspaper asking for people to speak with me about their school experiences. Despite the great article written about the project, it yielded just one response. It's been a terrific experience, albeit with one real disappointment: My vision for student involvement was to have them conduct some interviews that time wouldn't permit me to do, help with formatting photos for the book, and write their own chapter about their school experiences. They could have chronicled the sports, art, drama, and music programs in depth. The possibilities were endless. Despite my cajoling, wheedling, pleading, and meeting with school administrators, the result was zip, zero, nada. There would be no student component. It was a tremendous disappointment to me. Why?

A bit about me will answer that question. I attended BCSD schools for grades 2–12. I graduated in 1976, the year of our country's Bicentennial, when our biggest concern was whether we would have to wear red, white, and blue graduation gowns. In those days female graduates wore white, the male graduates wore royal blue. I have no idea why. We were just happy that red wasn't introduced into the equation.

I returned to BCHS in 1990 and spent the ensuing twenty-five years teaching English. It was an enjoyable part of my life. For students not to be involved with this project was a crushing blow. However, I did remember being that age and couldn't decide if I would have participated or not. I enjoyed history, so I probably would have volunteered to help with something. Current generations are more concerned with an extra grade or an event for a resume. Since this book is ultimately about students who gained a quality education due to the efforts of those early educational pioneers, I was sorry they wouldn't help in providing some payback.

I have reached the end of this road and I have said my piece. There are not enough words for me to express my gratitude to the teachers who provided me with a tremendous educational foundation. They also taught me to be intellectually curious, to ask questions, to be certain to have good examples to back my opinions. Most of all they taught me to respect myself and others.

Because collecting information for this book took several years, several people who took the time to speak with me have unfortunately since passed away. To a person, each was humble and passionate about the school district whether they were former students, teachers, or administrators, and I mourn their passing.

I would like to especially remember a handful of individuals who challenged me, believed in me, and exposed me to a world of wonder. They are (in no particular order): Mrs. Maria Crysler, Mrs. Elsa Gunther, Mr. Alfred Restifo, Mrs. Mary Woehrle, Mr. Warren Stoker, Mr.

Richard Nestlen, Mr. Richard Feldman, Mr. Ralph (Neil) Brown, Miss Marcy Stafford, Mr. Tom Hitchcock, Mr. Dominick DeCecco, Miss Margaret Dinova, Dr. Frank Madigan, Dr. Elaine Ognibene, Dr. Alexander Wheelock, and Dr. Eberhard Alsen.

My thoughts would not be complete unless I mentioned Mr. Donald Camp. Mr. Camp was a longtime English teacher at the high school and an epic tennis coach. I took tennis lessons from him in my early teenage years. He was a consummate gentleman, every inch a Renaissance man. He did not use words excessively, and each one had merit. After I began teaching English at BCHS, I would encounter him in the reading area of the Public Library. Our conversations extended to my teaching career and to our shared memories. Mr. Camp was a gifted athlete, proficient in tennis and golf. He was a tennis professional and club pro. He was not boastful. Men like this are rare and I was so lucky to know more than my fair share, especially through the work on this project. Their impact on my life is incredible.

During the time of the first fifty years of the school district, the United States was impacted by three wars: World War II, Korea, and Vietnam. War inevitably means loss of human life. I became "acquainted" with several who gave their lives. In more recent times I have lost three of my former students to war. It is my hope that some individual might take up their cause and document their stories on paper so they will not be forgotten.

Three wonderful resources provided me with the bulk of the information contained in this book. The first is the collection of the *Oriole* yearbooks. I can say with certainty that I have pored over each one. They are time capsules and capture the spirit of youth. The second is newspapers. Using digital databases and the New York State Library, I plowed through hundreds of newspaper articles. They are so beautifully written and informative, almost conversational at times. Their historic worth is immeasurable. Finally, to all of those with whom I've spoken over the years…this is my gift to you. This is your book. This is your story. You all played a huge part in the story of this school district's success. Our conversations will remain intact in my heart forever.

It was impossible to include everything I'd envisioned. Information for the early years of the district was hard to find and/or nonexistent. There were no records from Delmar or Clarksville Schools. There was a finite amount of time. I toyed with including some information about St. Thomas School but decided it should be its own project. For those who wanted to hear more about sports, music, or drama, or the impact of Mr. Richard Feldman on our drama program, I encouraged many of you to produce some information for me to include. It seems you "forgot" to send it to me. I had hoped for student involvement, but it seems that wasn't meant to be. In the words of the great writer Kurt Vonnegut, "So it goes."

Beth Anderson '76
Delmar, NY
August 11, 2023

N.B. Any errors contained in this book are my own.

BIBLIOGRAPHY

Bennett, Allison. "School days long ago." *Spotlight*, 14 August 1985, A5.

Bennett, Allison. *Times Remembered*. (Delmar: Newsgraphics of Delmar, Inc.): Allison Bennett, publisher, 1984.

Brewer, Floyd (ed.). *Bethlehem Revisited*. (Albany: Lane Press): Bethlehem Bicentennial Committee, 1993.

Community United Methodist Church: interview with members. Unpublished manuscript. 1979–1980.

Dickinson, Mrs. Paul E. "A Short History of Delmar, New York." *Albany County Post*, 21 Nov 1952.

Gazin, Sharon. "2 from the class of 1934 look back." *The Knickerbocker News*, 10 Mar 1983.

Gottesman, Bart. "In 61 years, Delmar has changed a lot." *Spotlight*. 27 Aug 1986, 18.

Hosey, Dorothy et al. "The Fiftieth Anniversary Celebration of the first high school graduating class of BCSD, 1984." Unpublished manuscript.

Porter, Alice. "Delmar Then and Now 1926-1974." Unpublished manuscript.

Shiebler, Howard A. "Bethlehem---a Bridge, a Stove and ---." *The Knickerbocker News*, 28 May 1957.

Treadway, Ann. "W. Jack Weaver...'Father' of Bethlehem School District." *The Helderberg Sun*, 23 May 1978.

NEWSPAPERS

The Albany County Post. Historic Newspapers. Fultonhistory.com/Fulton.html.

The Altamont Enterprise, July 1888 to December 2008. Historicnewspapers.guilpl.org.

The Knickerbocker News. Historic Newspapers. Fultonhistory.com/Fulton.html.

The Times Union. Historic Newspapers. Fultonhistory.com/Fulton.html.

INTERVIEWS AND PERSONAL RESOURCES

Andrew Baker

Jeanne Bonacker Baum '63

Heidi Bonacquist

Paul Bradley '63

Frederick Burdick

Barbara Castle '57

Benjamin Castle '55

Joyce Knighton Christianson '69

Miki Cunningham Conn '62

Alice Corbett

Dominick DeCecco

Albert Easton '56

Richard Feldman

Laura Heffernan

Judy Slingerland Kimes '68

Joanne Glenn Kimmey '44

Kate Kloss

Michael Klugman

David Ksanznak

Susan Hardy Leath

Randall Miller '76

William Morrison

John Murray '40

FitzEdward Otis '63

Richard Owen '63

Gertrude Prater
  (on behalf of Larry Prater)

Cheryl Randall
  (on behalf of John Randall '45)

Stanley Reich

Roberta Rice '65

Mary Richards

Betty Carlson Roxborough '44

Terry Stephany Royne '67

Joseph Schaefer

Sandy Paige Sorell
  (on behalf of Harry Paige '41)

Warren Stoker

Linda Camp Strebel '64

Rex Trobridge '62

Richard Vanderbilt '67

Rick Van Dusen

Cheryl Maxwell Vieira '62

John Yacobian '81

BIBLIOGRAPHY FOR THE WORK OF JOHN YACOBIAN

American Antiquarian Society, Harry and Grace Goddard, Website (https://www.americanatiquarian.org). Portraits in the American Antiquarian Society Worcester, MA

Spencer Wire Company Collection Harvard Business School, Baker Library Collection Women Enterprise and Society Collections Catalog Record, Mss 596 1876-1929 S745 Volume 1

Residential Building Lots Edwin C Heinsohn Property Hamagrael Park Albany County Clerk's Office, Filed May 21, 1937

Oral and written interviews conducted with Tina Pough, daughter of Raymond Heinsohn and Judy Heinsohn Quinn, daughter of Betsy Heinsohn Quinn, 2010

Charles Nutt, *History of Worcester and Its People* (New York: Lewis Publishing Co., 1919)

INDEX

numbers in italics indicate photos

A

Ableman, Dick, 60
Ableman, Edna, 59–60
Advanced Placement classes, 124–25
African American families, 119–20
Albany
    annexes part of Town of Bethlehem, 63, *64*
    passage to Delmar and Elsmere, 95
    Regents exams held in, 53–54
    train service between Delmar and, 11, 49, 129
    water supplied to, 79
Albany, State University at (formerly Albany Normal School), *4*
Albany Academy, 6
Albany and Susquehanna Railroad (currently the Delaware and Hudson Railroad), 49
Albany County Post, The, 38
Albany County Rail Trail, 49
Albany County Sheriff's Office, 47
Albany High School, 6, 11, 14, 52, *52*
Albany Normal School (now State University at Albany), *4*
Albany-Rensselaerville Plank Road (now New Scotland Road), 49
Albany Times Union, 20, 37–38, *37*, 42, 142
Alcove Reservoir, 79
Allen, Dean Brooks, 19–20, *19*
Allen, Florence, 19, *20*
Allen, Joyce, 20
"Alouette" (song), 54
Alpha Zeta fraternity, 141

Altamont Enterprise The
    on Bookhout, 99, 101
    on Clarksville School, 36
    on Delmar School District, 9, 15
    on Elsmere School District, 29, 31
    on funding for Slingerlands School, 54
    on sanitary conditions in Slingerlands School, 54
    on skating and sledding parties, 139
    Weaver on taxpayers and new school building, 96
American Antiquarian Society (AAS), 92, 93
Applebee Funeral Home, 18, 20
Architectural Forum, The, 42
auditorium
    at Delaware Avenue school, 111
    at Delmar School, 15, 134
    at Elsmere School, 30, 134
    at Slingerlands School, 54
Austin, Erwin, 139
Austin, Mr. (teacher at Glenmont School), 70
Austin, Richard, 139
auto shop, 105

B

Babcock's Corners (now Bethlehem Center), *62*, 63
Baker, Andrew, *60*
Ballston Spa School District, 120
bands, 133–34, *134*
band uniforms, 116, *116*
Bango, Anthony, *122*
Barracini's (store), 31
baseball teams, 11, *128*, 129

basketball, 132, *132*
bell system, 108
Benanati, Jenay, *69*
Bennett, Allison, 4–5
Beta Gamma Rho sorority, 140, 141
Bethlehem, Town of
    Albany annexes part of, 63, *64*
    authorizes centralization of schools, 7
    children can attend Delmar High School for free, 12
    comprised of many Common Schools, 14
    current owner of Cedar Hill Schoolhouse, 5
    date of incorporation, 1
    farming decreases in, 37
    hamlets comprising, 3
    and population growth, 95, 105
    religion in, 118–19
    town seal, viii
Bethlehem Archeology Group, 66–67
Bethlehem Center (formerly Babcock's Corners), *62*, 63
Bethlehem Center School, *64–66*, 65–68, 71
    cover of PTA program, *73*
    original, 63, *64*
    transitions to Glenmont Elementary School, 73
Bethlehem Central High School (BCHS)
    curriculum expansion at, 123–24
    expansion of, 124
    gymnasium at, *125*
    opening of, 111–12
    original floor plan, *110*
    ranking of, 125–27
    student life at, 129–47
    teachers and principals at, 112–23
    see also specific activities
Bethlehem Central Middle School, 108
Bethlehem Central School District (BCSD)
    acquires 18 acres of land, 92
    administrators, 98–101
    centralization and evolution of, 7
    Clarksville becomes part of, 35, 37
    on filling teacher vacancies, 114
    formation of, 16
Bethlehem Central Teacher's Association (BCTA), 120–24, *121–22*
Bethlehem Historical Association, 5

Bethlehem Preschool, 65
Bethlehem Public Library, 50, 54
Bethlehem Revisited (Brewer), 63, 105
Bethlehem Tennis Association, 132
Bethlehem Town Hall, 17, 25, 127
Bethlehem Turnpike (now NYS route 443), 35
Bethlehem White Christmas Festival, 117–18
Bible reading in school, 54
bicycling, 142–43, *143*
Bida, Mary, 61
bike safety program, *45*
Blatner, Henry, 38–39, *40*, 41–42
blind students, 77–78
Bonacker, George, 17, *25*
Bonacquist, Heidi, 61
bonfire, 144, *145*
Bookbinder, Harold, 109
Bookhout, Hamilton
    assists Jewish family, 118–19
    favors network of neighborhood schools, 40, 46
    as principal and superintendent, 55, 75, 76, 81, 99–101, *99*, *101*, 112
Bouck, Olin, 16, *16*, 37, 98, *98*, *126*
Boughton, Miss (teacher in Slingerlands School), 53
Bover, Roland "Ron," 23, *23*, 43–44, *44*
bowling alley, 140, *140*
Boy Scouts, 142–43, *143*
Boys' Life, 142
Bozzella, Sam, 116, *117*
Brewer, Floyd, 63
Brooklyn Dodgers, 31
Brown, Herman, 120, *120*
Brown, Mr. (teacher at Glenmont School), 70
Brown, Ralph, *121*
Browne, Dr. Harold, 33, 140
Burdick, Frederick, 108, *108*, 109
bus transportation, 14, 36

C

cafeteria
    in Elsmere School, 29
    lack of, in Slingerlands School, 55–56
    in new high school, 111

Camp, Don, 132–33, *132–33*
Cannon, *91*
the Canteen, 137, *138*, 139
Capp, Al, 143
Carrol, Andrew, *19*, 20
Cass, Etta, 33
Catholics, 118
CBS News, 93
Cedar Hill Schoolhouse (District #1), 5
census
    Federal (1920), 13
    school, 56
centralization
    and administrators for Bethlehem Central School District, 98
    and approval of new high school, 96
    and closure of Cedar Hill School, 5
    and formation of Bethlehem Central School District, 16
    and growth of district enrollment, 76
    map of schools prior to centralization, 2
    in New Scotland, 36
    teachers required to live within Town of Bethlehem, 32–33
    Weaver advocate for, 6, 7, 95
Chapman, Roslyn, *126*
Chase, Professor, 13
Chesser, Doug, 142, *143*
Christian Brothers Academy, 6
Circus presentation, 68, *69–70*
City of Athens (ship), 87
Civil War, 63
Clarksville School (District #2)
    bike safety program at, *45*
    Bover and outdoor education curriculum at, 23
    closed in June 2011, 44
    experimental educational programs in, 44
    Falvey principal at, 76, 80
    future expansion of, 42–43, *43*
    map of Clarksville (1886), *34*
    new school design, *40–41*, *43*
    Restifo teacher at, 27
    Schaefer as principal at, 80
    students at old school, *36*
    and teachers' labor dispute, 122
    used for community events, 42
clerestory windows, 42

Clermont (steamship), 5
coal stoves and gas, 37–38, *37–38*
Coates, Ruth Wheeler, *10*
Cold War, 106, 113
Colonie school districts, 83
Common Schools
    in Clarksville, 35
    establishment of, 3
    and financial independence of, 63
    growing obsolescence of, 7, 36
    limitations of, 5–6
    in Slingerlands, 50
compulsory education, 3, 35
Conn, Miki Cunningham, 119–20, *119*
continuing education for teachers, 114
Coons, Heth, 16, *16*, 98–99, *99*
Cornell University, 145
Cortland College, 44
Coughtry, Helen Earl, 50, 52
crest on school ring, 146, *147*
Cronin (former teacher at Delmar Elementary School), 17
Crysler, Maria, 17
curriculum
    Advanced Placement classes, 124–25
    creativity in, 82–83
    electives in, 123–24
    expansion of, in Delaware Avenue school, 115
    experimental high school in Delmar, 12, *12*, 13
    music added to, 98, 108, 111, 115-16, 133
    outdoor education curriculum, 23–24, *24*, 43–44, 68
    physical education in, 28
Currie, Mildred, *126*
custodians, 55, 70
Cut-Rite wax paper sandwich bags, 31, *31*

D

dairy farming, 35
Daisy Mae Drag, 143–44, *144*
dances and dancing, 24, 28, 31, 133 , 134, 139, 141, 143–44, *144*
Daniels, F. Harold, 87
Delaware and Hudson Railroad (formerly the Albany and Susquehanna Railroad), 49
Delaware Avenue (older), *29*

Delaware Avenue bridge, 6
Delaware Gardens, 32, *32*
Del Lanes, 140
Delmar Department Store, 23
Delmar Fire House, 23
Delmar Game Farm (now Five Rivers), 23
Delmar Lions Club, 79
Delmar Men's Orchestra, 116–17
Delmar School (District # 10)
    Borthwick Avenue site chosen for first high school, 14–15, *15*
    curriculum under Smith, 17–18
    early Delmar School, *8*
    elementary school closes, 17, 25
    formation of, 16–17
    as foundation of school district, 24
    gymnasium and auditorium in, 15, 134
    high school baseball team, *128*
    high school becomes Delmar Elementary, 127
    high school curriculum, experimental, 12, *12*, 13
    high school first graduating class, 126–27, *126*,
    high school opens 1926-27 school year, 6
    high school retains name for only 6 years, 16
    houses Glenmont elementary students, 65
    J. Herrmann teaches at, 29
    junior high before cafeteria addition, *130*
    limitations of new, 10–11, *10*
    "never be filled," 76
    overcrowding in, 13–14, 75
    residents vote to replace original, 9–10, *10*
    Schaefer as principal at, 80
    Schaefer on closing of, 81
    situated in neighborhoods, 79
Delmar Theater, 134, *135*
Delmar Train Station, *11*, *128*
Delta Psi sorority, 140
DePorte, Katie, 61
Dibble, Cary, *70*
domestic science, 12
Dorsey, Pat, *45*
Dulles, John Foster, 115
Dunlap, Ellen, 92

E

eagle (mascot), 145
Eagle Elementary School, 46
Earth Day, 66
Edmonds, Mrs. (teacher at Glenmont School), 70
electives, 124
"Elmarion" (Goddard house in Worcester), 90
Elsmere, hamlet of, *30*
Elsmere School (District #15) (1911-1929)
    additions to, 29, 37–38
    auditorium in, 30, 134
    community events held at, 31
    former students' memories of, 30–33
    as foundation of school district, 24
    gymnasium in, 28, 134
    high school opens, 28
    houses Glenmont elementary students, 65
    last graduating class, *33*
    last of one-room schoolhouses in Bethlehem, 27
    library in, 29
    "never be filled," 76
    new, 28, *28*
    original school and class with Mrs. Sexton, *26*
    overcrowding in, 75
    picketing by teachers at, *122*
    Robillard teaches at, 73
    situated in neighborhoods, 79
environmental education, 23–24, *24*
Erkson, Grace, 65–66, *67*, 71

F

factories and factory workers, 52
    Spencer Wire Company, 85, 87
    wages of, 52
Fairbank, Jack, 142, *142*
fallout shelters, 106, *106*
Falvey, John, 77, 80, *80*
farmers and farming
    across from Glenmont School, 66
    Bethlehem at beginning of 20th century, 1

curriculum for study at Delmar High
School, 12
dairy, 35
decrease of, in Bethlehem and New
Scotland, 37
dwindling of, 7
effect upon school attendance, 3
Future Farmers of America (FFA), 98
Hamagrael Farm, 88–90, *89*
Schiffendecker Farm Preserve, 67
scientific, 12
Slingerlands began as settlement of
farms, 49
Stephens farm purchased for
Delaware Avenue school, 111
Weaver evaluates agricultural
education programs, 95
Farrell, Joseph, 116, *116*
Federal Census (1920), 13
Feldman, Richard, 147
Feller, Debbie, *55*
Feura Bush Road, 63, 67, 73, 79
Five Rivers (formerly Delmar Game Farm), 23
Foley, Dee, *55*
football, 130–31, *130-31*
Ford, Susan, *69*
Four Corners, 10, 23
fraternities, 140–42. *see also specific
fraternities*
Frazier, Evelyn, 52
Fuller, Mrs. (teacher at Glenmont School), 70
Future Farmers of America (FFA), 98

G

Gainor, Dr., 33
Gamma Rho sorority, 140
Ganey, Santa, 116
Geurtze, Harold, 137
Giombetti, Dr., 33
Glenmont School
aerial photo of, *68*
Bethlehem Center School transitions
to, 73
building of Glenmont Elementary, 65
Circus participants, 68, *69–70*
Falvey as principal of, 80
"Family Night Movie Theatre," 67
new building completed May 1957, 66

PTA and school scholarship, 72
students assist Bethlehem
Archeology Group, 66–67
and teachers' labor dispute, 122
third grade class picture, *71*
unique location of, 66, 67
Glenn, John, 76
glider construction, *104*, 105
Goddard family
Eleanor, *86*, 87, 90
Grace Watson, *86*, 87, 90
Harry, 85, *86*, 87, 90
home in Worcester, MA, 90, 92
Marion, *86*, 87, 90
photo credits, 93
Robert, 87
summer home basis of name
Hamagrael, 90
see also Heinsohn family
Great Depression, 75, 90, 102
Guilderland District, 80, 108
Gunther, Elsa, 17, 23
gymnasium
at Bethlehem Central High School, *125*
at Clarksville School, 43
at Delaware Avenue high school, 111,
124, *125*
at Delmar School, 15, 134
at new Elsmere School, 28, 134
at Slingerlands School, 54

H

Half Moon (Henry Hudson's flagship), viii,
146, *147*
Hall, Marge, 88
Hamagrael
Hamagrael Park, *74*, 75, 90, *91*, 92
origin of name, 75, 85–92
unique location of, 79
Hamagrael Farm, 88–90, *89*, 93
Hamagrael School
built to accommodate overflow from
Delmar and Elsmere, 75–76, *76*, 79
design of classrooms, 81–82
elementary, *84*
elementary school nicknamed
"Hamajail," 82, 85
Erkson teaches at, 71

159

how school was named, 85–92
    mainstreaming at, 77–78
    playground behind, *81*
Harrington, Dondrue, 55
Harris, Tom, 142, *142*
Hasselbarth, Harold, 142, *142*
Hasselbarth, Tom, 142, *142*
Hauser family, 56–58
    Doug, *57–58*
    Scott, 56, *58*
Healey, Steve, *70*
Heicklen, Muriel, *78*
Heilmann, Henry, *70*
Heinsohn family
    Barbara, 89, *90–91*
    Edwin, 88, *88*, 90, *91*, 92
    Elizabeth Hall, *88*, 88–89, *90–91*, 92
    Judith Quinn, 88, *90–91*, 92
    Meredith, 89, *90–91*
    photo credits, 93
    Raymond, 89, *90–91*, 92
    see also Goddard family
Heldeberg Workshop, 44, 58, *60*
Herrmann, Jeanne, 29
Herrmann, Richard, 29, 30
Hobbie, Helen, 113
Hodgkinson, Rebecca Hauser, 56, *58*
Holmes, Thomas, 12
Homecoming, 144
Hosey, Dorothy, 17–18, 22–23, *22*,
Hosey, Gladys, 114–15, *114*
Howe, Mrs. (teacher at Glenmont School), *71*
Howes, Kimball, 113
Hudson, Henry, viii, 146, *147*
Hungerford, Bernie, 61
Hungerford, Frank, 14
Hungerford, Muriel, 61

I

Images of America - Bethlehem (Leath), 50
indigenous populations, 85
Irons, Clyde, 55
Ives, Sammie, 82–83, *82*

J

jackets for fraternities, *141*

Japan, 23
Jasper's corner store, 23
Jensen, Connie, *122*
jewelry
    D. Mc Donald's pins, 46, *46*
    school ring, 146
Jewish families, 118–19
junior high schools *vs.* middle schools, 106–9

K

Kallop, Jean, 55
Kennedy, John F., 23, 57–58
Kenwood Avenue School (District #12)
    Albany absorbs Kenwood area, 63, *64*
    auto shop in, 105
    double sessions for students, 102, 105–6, 111
    early view of Kenwood Avenue campus, *100*
    glider construction class, *104*, 105
    murals in, 106
    new junior/senior high school, 97, *102–3*
    proposed additions, *107*
    voters reject funds for new high school, 96, *96*
kindergarten
    at Bethlehem Center School, 65, 68
    pre-kindergarten program at Clarksville, 44
    at Slingerlands Methodist Church, 65
    at Slingerlands School, 54
Kinsley, William, 101, *101*, 106
Knapp, David, 135
Knickerbocker News, The, 77–78, 120
Knowles, Helen, *126*
Korean War, 22
Ksanznak, Dave, 82
Kunz, Walter "Jimmie," 10

L

laboratory schools, 3–4
"La Cucaracha" (song), 54
Lawson's Lake, 23, *24*, 43, 68
Leath, Susan, 50

Legion Hall, 27
Lenhardt, Lynne, *56*
Leonard, Lt. John, *79*
Lephart, Clarence, 147
Lewis, Pamela, *69*
library
    at Clarksville school, 43
    at Delaware Avenue school, 111
    at Elsmere School, 29
    use of, to prepare research papers, 115
Liebl, Wendy Hauser, *56, 58*
Life magazine, 116–17
lighting innovations, *43*
Li'l Abner comic strip, 143
lime-burning, 35
Lindsay, Dorothy, *70*
liquor, 40
Little Red Schoolhouse, 5
Long, Frances, 41
Lowe, Virginia, 61
lunches
    lunch recess, 70
    no kitchen for lunch preparation at Slingerlands, 55–56
Lutkus, Evonne, *55*, 61
Lutzen, John, 135

M

mainstreaming, 77
March of Dimes, 141
Marston, Alfred, 145
Marston, Elizabeth, 145
Masonic Temple, 9, 16, 17, 98
Massachusetts
    first state to require compulsory education of children, 3
Massachusetts Institute of Technology (MIT), 38
McDonald, Dorothy, 44, 46, *46*
McGuffey, William Holmes, 77
McGuffey Readers, 77, *77*
mechanical arts, 12
Methodist Church, 50, 54, 65, 118
middle schools *vs.* junior high schools, 106–9
Milner, Sally Hauser, *56, 58*

Milne School, *4*, 6, 11, 52
model railroading, *142*
Modern Movement, 39
Mohawk Hudson Land Conservancy, 67
molding sand, 1
Momberger, Lisa, *69*
Moomaw, Richard, 109
Morrison, William, 57–59, *59*
movies, 134
Murphy, Dave, 44, *45, 56*, 61, 80, 109
music and musicals
    music added to curriculum, 98, 108, 111, 115–16, 133
    music for school's alma mater, 145
    at Slingerland School, 57, *58*

N

National Foundation for the Blind, 79
Neff, Ken, 147
Neuthardt, Emerson, 105, *105*
Newell, Gladys, 113–14, *113*, 123
New Scotland
    farming decreases in, 37
    map, *34*
    school district, 35–36
    see also Voorheesville
New Scotland Road (formerly Albany-Rensselaerville Plank Road), 49
New York City, 67
New York State
    establishes normal schools, 3
    passes legislation leading to education reforms, 35
New York State Education Department, 95, 108
New York State Museum, 23
New York State Thruway, 67
New York Yankees, 31
Nicoll farm, 4
Niskayuna School District, 108
normal schools, 3–4
Normanside Country Club, 140
Normanskill Creek, 63, *64*, 95
Normansville School (District #11), 27
North and South Colonie districts, 123
NYS route 443 (formerly Bethlehem Turnpike), 35

O

O'Brien, Leo, 22
Oliver, Mr. and Mrs. Vernon, 17, 21–23, *21*
"Open Classroom" program, 44
orchestras, 115–16, 133, *134*
Oriole (yearbook)
    ad for war bonds, *104*, 105
    Bouck in first issue of, *16*
    on Delaware Avenue school, 112
    Delmar students in, 36
    origin of name, 145–46, *146*
O'Shea, Bonnie, *59*
outdoor education program, 23–24, *24*, 43–44, 68
outhouses, 2
Owen, Dick, *143*

P

Palumbo, Anita, *114*
parades, 144–45
Pardoe, Marcie, *67*, 70
Paro, Wilfred, 112, *113*
Parry, George, 70–71
pep rally, 144, *145*
Phi Delta Phi fraternity, 140, *141*
physical education
    lack of, in public schools, 11
    national movement for, 28
    see also gymnasium
Pittz, Karl, *70*
plane spotters, 105
plank roads, 49
Plattsburgh Press-Republican, 21
Plattsburgh State (now SUNY Plattsburgh), 83
playground, *81*
Poplaski, Rick, *121*
Pough, Tina, 92
prayer services in school, 54
pre-kindergarten program, 44
principals
    Erkson as district's first female, 71
    salaries for, 52
private academies, 3
Protestant Work Ethic, 118

PTAs (Parent Teacher Associations)
    handbook from Glenmont School, 71, *72–73*
    lack of, at Slingerlands, 50

Q

Quinn, Betsy, 92

R

railroads. *see* train travel
Ravena, 11, 129
Reformed Church, 118
Regents exams, 53–54
research papers, 115
Restifo, Alfred, 27, *27*, *122*
Revolutionary War, 79
Rexford, Lillian, *126*
Riggio, Tona, *122*
Rivkin family, 137
Robillard, Donald, 71, 73, *73*
roller rink, 140, *140*
Roosevelt, Franklin Delano, 102
Rothaupt, Karen, *122*
Rounds, Charlotte, *55*
Route 9W, 67, 73
Rugg, Richard, 137, *137*
Runge, Paul, 113

S

sabbaticals, 113
Sadie Hawkins Dance, 143–44, *144*
Saint, Eva Marie, 118, *118*
Samuelson, Miss (teacher at Glenmont School), 70
Schaefer, Joseph, 44, 80–81
Schenectady School District, 120
Schiffendecker Farm Preserve, 67, *69*
scholarships, 70–71, *72*
school census, 56
school children
    attendance issues, 3
    bus transportation for, 14
    compulsory education of, 3

school district
    definition of, 1
school ring, 146
schools
    centralization of, 6, 7, 16
    map of, prior to centralization, 2
    see also Common Schools
school taxes, 52
school tickets for train fare, 52
Scurrah, Thomas, 145
Sexton, Mettie, 26, 27, 33
Seymour Packing Company, 88
Sigma Kappa Delta fraternity, 140, 141, *141*
Sigma Theta Epsilon sorority, 140
singing, 54, 83, 133
skating, 90, 139–40
sledding, 134–35
Slingerlands
    began as settlement of working farms, 49
    railroads important to development of, 49
Slingerlands Methodist Church, 50, 65
Slingerlands Players, 79
Slingerlands School (District #9), 49–61, *51, 53, 60*
    auditorium in, 54
    as "A Very Special Place," *60*, 61
    and closure of Clarksville school, 46
    common school in, 50
    expansion at, 76
    funding for, 54
    houses Glenmont elementary students, 65
    lack of kitchen for lunch preparation, 55–56
    lack of PTAs at, 50
    musicals in, 57, *58*
    nicknames for, 55
    prayers and Bible reading in, 54
    salaries for teachers and principals in, 52
    sanitary conditions in, 54
    75th anniversary celebration, *56–59*
    situated in neighborhoods, 79
    stability of principals in elementary schools, 61
    students at Albany High, 52
    teachers conduct school census for, 56
Slingerlands Train Station, *50*

Sliter, Ray, 147
Smith, Arlington F., 17–19, *18*, 29, 33
Smith, Florence (Flossie), 17, 19, 20, *20*, 29
Smith, Harold, 113
Smith, James, 54–55, 61
Smith, Tommy, 77
Smith, Violet, *126*
Smitty (custodian), 70
snow glare, 42
social clubs, 135, *136*
sororities, 140–42. see also specific sororities
special education, 83
Spelich, Virginia Dale, 57, *58*
Spencer Wire Company, 85, 87
Sporthaven Lanes, 140
Spotlight, The, 10, 70, 117–18
Stephany, Ray, 42–43, 44
Stephens farm, 111
Stoker, Warren, 122
Stratton, Samuel, 22
St. Stephen's Church, 27
suburbs
    Delaware Gardens, 32, *32*
    families relocating to, 6–7, 11, 28, 37
    in Hamagrael Park, *74*, 75–76
Suez Canal Crisis, 115
SUNY Plattsburgh (formerly Plattsburgh State), 83
swimming pool, 76, 111, *112*
Syracuse University, 55, 60

T

Tappa Kega Beer (TKB) fraternity, 140, *141*
Tau Epsilon Psi fraternity, 140, *141*
taxes, 52
teachers
    assigned to take school census in Slingerlands, 56
    continuing education for, 114
    former, at Slingerlands School, *55*
    normal schools as preparation for, 3–4
    picketing by, 120–22, *121–22*
    preparing for middle school model, 107–9
    qualifications for in New York State, 124

required to live within Town of Bethlehem, 32–33
responsibilities of, 1–3, 11
salaries for, 52
specialized instruction for mainstreaming students, 78–79
teachers' union, 114
Teeling, George, 38
telephone exchange, *134*
tennis, 131–32, *133*
Terhune, Donald Z., *97*, 98
theater program, 147
Title IX, 147
Tlingit tribe, 119
tobacco, 40
Toll Gate Restaurant, *48*, 49
tolls and tollgates, *48*, 49, 67–68
Tompkins, Virgil, 113
Town Court, 25
Township School Act (1917), 12, 13
train travel
    Delmar Train Station, *128*
    importance in development of Slingerlands, 49
    importance in development of Tri-Village area, 27–28
    and population expansion to suburbs, 6–7, 11
    school tickets for, 52
    students' use of, 129
    for Voorheesville students, 36
Tri Hi-Y, 135, *136*
Tri-Village area, 27–28
Tri-Village Directory, *140*
Trobridge, Rex, 60
Truitt, Rolland, 116–17, *118*, 133, *133*
Tudico, Nancy, 70–71, *72*

U

"Ungraded" program, 44
Union Classical Institute, 141
Union College, 141
Union Free School District (UFSD), 14
US News and World Report, 125

V

Van Dyke, Leon, and the Brothers, 120
Vietnam War, 20

Voorheesville
    Sheriff's Office outgrows office in, 47
    students from Clarksville sent to, 36–37
    students take train to Delmar to attend school in, 129

W

Wagner, Glenn, 142–43, *143*
war bonds, *104*, 105
War Letters: Extraordinary Letters from American Wars (Carroll), 19, 20
the "water line," 79
Watervliet High School, 73
Weaver, W. Jack, 6, 7, *94*, 95–96
Weiss, Mrs. (teacher at Bethlehem Center School), 68
Whipple, Jack, 147
Whitman, Governor, 12, 13
Whitney, Dorothy, 30, 44
Williams, Hugh, 17, 23, *24*
Wilson, Tom, *143*
Wiltsey, Mrs. (teacher at Glenmont School), 67
window boxes, 42
Winship, Tommy, 78, *78*
Woodside School, *39*
Worcester, Massachusetts, 85
Worcester Antiquarian Society, 90
World Series, 30–31
World War II
    expansion of suburbs after, 92
    impact upon high school students, 102, *104*, 105
    Morrison's service during, 58
Wynkoop property, 139

Y

Yacobian, John, 75, 85, 92–93
yearbooks
    curriculum expansion reflected in, 115
    emblem, *127*
    see also the *Oriole*
York, Magdalene, 116, *117*
youth center, 134–35, 137, *138*, 139